MVFOL

PERSONAL LEARNING NETWORKS

WILL RICHARDSON
ROB MANCABELLI

Solution Tree | Press

a division of

Solution Tree

555 North Morton Street
Bloomington, IN 47404
800.733.6786 (toll free) / 812.336.7700
FAX: 812.336.7790

email: info@solution-tree.com
solution-tree.com

Visit **go.solution-tree.com/technology** to access the links in this book.

Printed in the United States of America
15 14 13 12 11   1 2 3 4 5

FSC

Mixed Sources
Product group from well-managed
forests and other controlled sources

Cert no. SW-COC-002283
www.fsc.org
© 1996 Forest Stewardship Council

Library of Congress Cataloging-in-Publication Data

Richardson, Will.
    Personal learning networks : using the power of connections to transform education / Will Richardson, Rob Mancabelli.
        p. cm.
    Includes bibliographical references and index.
    ISBN 978-1-935543-27-5 (perfect bound) -- ISBN 978-1-935543-28-2 (library edition) 1. Professional learning communities. 2. Internet in education. I. Mancabelli, Rob. II. Title.
    LB1731.R53 2011
    371.33'44678--dc22
                                2011013068

Solution Tree
Jeffrey C. Jones, CEO & President

Solution Tree Press
President: Douglas M. Rife
Publisher: Robert D. Clouse
Vice President of Production: Gretchen Knapp
Managing Production Editor: Caroline Wise
Copy Editor: Rachel Rosolina
Text and Cover Designer: Jenn Taylor

To Wendy, Tess, and Tucker for supporting me and encouraging me to follow my passions. I love you all. —Will Richardson

To my parents, Bob and Toni, for all of your love and support; and to my wife, Gayle, for sharing my life. —Rob Mancabelli

ACKNOWLEDGMENTS

First and foremost, we want to thank the educators whose stories we share in this book for having the courage, intelligence, and vision to transform your beliefs into practice. Also, thanks to Mark Klassen for letting us share his remarkable story. We want to thank everyone who read our work in its many forms, particularly El-ad David Amir and Dave Rossell, who provided invaluable insights throughout the writing process. Thanks also to the folks at Solution Tree who made the process a terrific experience, especially Robb Clouse, Kirsten Caster, Chelsea Gurney, and Gretchen Knapp.

Finally, it would be impossible to conclude without thanking the thousands of people in our learning networks. It is you who have made this book possible. Every idea here has been shaped not only by the authors that we admire, but by millions of blog posts, tweets, comments, YouTube videos, and podcasts that enrich our understanding of education around the globe every day. Thank you to every person who has taken the time out of their busy day to share experiences, knowledge, and understanding with the rest of the world. You enrich and honor our profession.

Solution Tree Press would like to thank the following reviewers:

Susan Brooks-Young
Author and Consultant
S.J. Brooks-Young Consulting
Lopez Island, Washington

William M. Ferriter
Sixth-Grade Teacher
Salem Middle School
Apex, North Carolina

John L. Brown
Supervisor, Curriculum Design
 and Resources
Alexandria City Public Schools
Alexandria, Virginia

Douglas Fisher
Professor, Department of Teacher
 Education
San Diego State University
San Diego, California

Caryn Cook
Curriculum Coordinator
Warren East High School
Bowling Green, Kentucky

Brad Flickinger
Technology Teacher
Bethke Elementary
Timnath, Colorado

Terry Cook
Principal
South Warren High School
Bowling Green, Kentucky

David Jakes
Coordinator of Instructional
 Technology
Glenbrook South High School
Glenview, Illinois

Gregory W. Lineweaver
Dean of Faculty, Assistant Head of
  School
Herron High School
Indianapolis, Indiana

Angela Maiers
Author, Speaker, Consultant
Maiers Educational Services
Clive, Iowa

Scott McLeod
Associate Professor, Educational
  Administration, and Director,
  CASTLE
Iowa State University
Ames, Iowa

Meg Ormiston
Author and Consultant
Tech Teachers, Inc.
Burr Ridge, Illinois

Jeff Utecht
Technology and Learning
  Coordinator
International School Bangkok
Nonthaburi, Thailand

TABLE OF CONTENTS

ABOUT THE AUTHORS

A parent of two middle school–aged children, **Will Richardson** has been writing about the intersection of social online learning networks and education since 2001 at www.weblogg-ed.com and in numerous journals and magazines such as *Ed Leadership*, *Education Week*, and *English Journal*. He was a public school educator for twenty-two years and is a cofounder of Powerful Learning Practice (www.plpnetwork.com), a unique professional development program that has mentored over three thousand teachers worldwide. His first book, *Blogs, Wikis, Podcasts and Other Powerful Web Tools for Classrooms* (3rd edition, 2010) has sold over 75,000 copies and has impacted classroom practice around the world. He has spoken to tens of thousands of educators in over a dozen countries about the merits of learning networks for personal and professional growth. He is a national advisory board member of the George Lucas Education Foundation and a regular columnist for *District Administration Magazine*. He lives with his wife, Wendy, and his children, Tess and Tucker, in rural Western New Jersey.

With nearly twenty years of experience in educational leadership, technology, and planning, **Rob Mancabelli** partners with schools, universities, and corporations to develop 21st century learning organizations. Since 2003, Rob has inspired audiences around the world with insights into the change process, strategies for engaging stakeholders, and methods for transforming organizations to meet the rapidly evolving demands of a globally connected world. A former CIO and certified PMP, he writes for numerous publications such as *School CIO* magazine, as well as at www.mancabelli.com; serves on K–12 advisory boards for Dell Computer and Acer Corporation; and is in the process of completing his MBA at MIT. Rob lives with his wife, Gayle Allen, in New York City.

To book Will Richardson or Rob Mancabelli for professional development, contact pd@solution-tree.com.

THE POWER OF NETWORKED LEARNING

Mark Klassen is a cinematographer with a growing reputation for creating beautiful videos. His work shows a great sense of framing, movement, and perspective—all the qualities on which compelling filmmaking is built. His videos reflect a wide range of topics: musical interpretations, wedding stories, documentaries, and sports. In 2010, in fact, he found himself on the sidelines of two New York Jets playoff games, capturing snippets from the game action, the crowd that was watching, and players in the locker room, much of which was seen by millions of people the following week on the NFL Network. He's won competitions, received awards, and has a growing list of clients who seek out his skills.

Not bad for a seventeen-year-old high school senior who's never had a minute of traditional classroom instruction in his chosen craft.

Mark's education around his passion for creating video has been built on a healthy mix of apprenticeship, experimentation, and self-direction. He's learned much working at the feet of other artists in and around his home near Toronto through volunteering and internships, but he also honed his skills with the help of people far away from Ontario, people he's never met face to face, never spoken to, and probably never will—people who share his love of video and want to help him become even better. Since 2009, he's become a part of an expanding global network of cinematographers online with whom he interacts on a regular basis.

Put simply, Mark is connected through his personal learning network (PLN). Through the readers and commenters on his blog at www .markaklassen.com, the 750 followers he has on his Twitter feed (@markklassen), and the over one hundred connections he's made on his Vimeo video-sharing page (www.vimeo.com/markklassen), he's immersed in an ongoing conversation about video making, about his work, and about his self-made education. Resources to help him perfect his craft abound online; he can learn about software like Final Cut Studio and Adobe Photoshop through online tutorials at sites such as www.lynda.com, all the while collaborating with others to dissect and deconstruct the work of more seasoned professionals at the many video sharing sites that he frequents regularly.

But it's his own willingness to put himself out there, to share his own work with the world, that provides the real payback.

"Sharing my work online so that other people can see it and give me feedback and advice on it has become a huge part of the way I learn," Mark says. "It's inspiring and motivating that so many people are willing to help push my thinking and my skills online. There are dozens of other artists I can count on to answer questions, share ideas, and make me see my own work in a different way. And those connections make it possible for me to gain a bigger audience, which means more feedback and more learning. A lot more people are finding me now" (M. Klassen, personal communication, January 14, 2011).

Welcome to learning in a networked world.

Right Here, Right Now

Right now, assuming we have an Internet connection, we can start to create a personal learning network—a set of connections to people and resources both offline and online who enrich our learning—at a moment's notice. With a PLN, we can learn anytime, anywhere, with potentially anyone around the world who shares our passion or interest. We can literally build global, online classrooms of our own making on the web that include networks and communities of learners with whom we interact on a regular basis. We can learn around a particular topic at a particular time, or simply tap into an ongoing stream of knowledge from which we can sip anytime we like. And we can build things together, things that can have a global impact in ways that were impossible only a few years ago. As Kansas State professor Michael Wesch describes it, we're entering a world marked by "ubiquitous computing, ubiquitous information, ubiquitous networks, at unlimited speed, about everything, everywhere, from anywhere, on all kinds of devices that make it ridiculously easy to connect, organize, share, collect, collaborate and publish" (TEDxTalks, 2010b). It's learning on demand, and for those like Mark Klassen who are already participating, it's quite an amazing place to be.

The Internet now connects us in unprecedented ways. We have social networks like Facebook and MySpace where millions of us share snippets of our lives with friends, family, and selected others. More importantly, we also have tools to go beyond the social, to connect with people we may not already know but who may quickly become mentors or collaborators, to create things with them, help change the world, or simply learn something new. These tools—like blogs, Twitter, social bookmarks, and many, many more—extend our reach into global conversations via text, audio, and video. In essence, they allow us to build global learning networks where, like Mark, we can pursue our intellectual or creative passions or needs with others who share them.

Make no mistake: it is passion that drives these connections, and that is the foundation for the *personal* learning networks we discuss in depth in this book. In our PLNs, we learn what we want or need to learn using the vast resources and people online (or off) that can help us learn it. Unlike traditional learning environments, each of our networks is unique, created and developed to our personalized learning goals that evolve and grow throughout our lives. For example, an educator's personal learning network might consist of communities of teachers sharing advice on proven approaches to curriculum and instruction, experts from various industries who interact with her classes on projects, and students from around the world invited into her classes to enrich her own students' perspectives.

It is, we think, an exciting new world of learning. As educators, however, we know these networked opportunities present us with a very big challenge. That's because schools have a long history of being the primary learning places in our children's lives. They have been an integral part, along with families and community, of a decidedly local learning network, one that still rules the day—at least for now. Students receive the bulk of their formal education from teachers who are often the sole source of reviewing student progress and suggesting paths for growth. They learn en masse with other students from their communities in the privacy of the school walls. It's a system that hasn't changed much since it was invented over a century ago.

But it is going to change. It has to, because the explosion of learning outside of school walls is too powerful to ignore. In fact you could say that at this moment, modern learning is shifting to the web. That's a big statement, we know, and we aim to prove our case. But make no mistake; the idea of schooling as we currently know it will struggle to remain relevant in a networked world. Let's be clear—that doesn't mean schools are going away anytime soon; they're not, and we're not advocating for it. We believe that schools and classrooms and local teachers have an incredibly important role to play in each child's learning. We believe in the relationships that children form with adults and in the dozens of other good things that happen every day in schools. Yet we're just as convinced that schools need to plug into this vibrant worldwide network of learning to stay relevant and to prepare our children for a vastly different learning landscape. That means schools will need to embrace a form of learning that is fundamentally different from the one they have known. This is not a case for education "reform" in the sense that we need only to make the current system perform better as measured by traditional methods, such as standardized tests. No, to prepare students to flourish in this new learning world, schools will need to *transform* themselves in important ways to become places where deep learning, inquiry, collaboration, and performance are the emphasis, not just test scores. We believe that personal learning networks are at the heart of this shift, and this book is a road map for that transformation.

It's Not About Reform; It's About *Transform*

We need only look outside of education to know that simple reforms are not going to cut it in a world where we can connect and create and share through the devices we carry in our pockets. Instead of reforming the education system—tweaking what we've got—we need to transform it—creating a new approach altogether. Ask politicians if the campaign and election process is being *reformed* by social networks that foster discussion and fundraising in new and important ways, and they'll tell you that this is not simply an improvement on the old system; it's a totally new system. Ask doctors, businessmen, musicians, and others about reform, and they'll tell you that the shifts since the turn of the 21st century are *transforming* their industries, that the structures and interactions within those industries are in many ways wholly new, not just tweaks on the old. They'll also tell you that the scale and the speed at which these changes and challenges are happening are unprecedented.

Take newspapers, for example. Like schools, newspapers have a successful model that has spanned hundreds of years. While the industry shifted slightly from decade to decade, for the most part the central core of the business remained unchanged: deliver well-written stories to large numbers of people in a paper format, and in return receive money from subscribers and advertisers. When the Internet arrived in the mid-1990s and threatened this model, most owners of the major papers were hesitant to respond. They tweaked it here and there, making small changes to adapt to the Internet age. Others took a different route, and instead of instituting changes, they came up with reasons why their industry was unique and would not be affected. A few who had been in the industry for decades told stories of how doomsayers had predicted the death of newspapers when radio came along, and then again when television arrived on the scene. "We'll be fine," they said. After all, it's a model that worked from the time of Ben Franklin to the time of Ben Bradlee.

But then it didn't work at all (see Roblimo, 2005). In a matter of a few years, the Internet began siphoning off readers and advertisers, subscriptions slowed, profits fell through the floor, and several high-profile papers closed their doors forever. From the advent of the web in the mid-1990s, newspaper circulation steadily declined from over 60 million to approximately 40 million (Ahrens, 2009; Newspaper Association of America, 2011). By the 2000s, many owners and management teams of individual newspapers pushed aside the rationalizations and excuses, making radical changes to try to survive. By then it was too late for most papers. Internet readers had already been going to other sources for years, and the opportunities for newspapers to embed their business model into the fabric of the Internet in innovative ways had passed them by. Now, for most papers, it's a waiting game as each year their subscribers dwindle and their advertising revenues decrease. In the long run only a handful may survive, and those that do may look nothing like they look today. Now it's sites like the *Huffington Post*, Gawker, and Talking Points Memo that are creating the new models for success in the Internet world.

The moral here is not a lesson in caution but rather a lesson to the cautious. It's not that newspapers didn't understand the threat; some did. It's not that some didn't try to make the web a part of their business. Actually, several newspaper leaders tried different ways of making their old model work in a new Internet-enabled world. The lesson here is how they framed the change. Newspapers continued to try to do what they had always done—in effect, trying to *adapt the Internet to them*. They tried to take the same content, produced by the same people, in the same ways, and get subscribers and advertisers to pay for it on the web in a traditional model. They tried to tweak their model and make small changes to survive in the Internet age. They did this partially because of excuses and inertia, but mostly because their vision of the past obscured their ability to invent a radically different future. Like most who try to fit old models into new paradigms, they failed. In short, newspapers refused to transform.

We believe education is following a similar path, trying to take the old model of schooling and adapt the technology to it. It's an understandable response, but it falls far short of using the power of these networks. The wake-up call for educators is not going to come from disappointing quarterly reports and falling revenues. If we continue to follow a safe and familiar path, our clarion call for change will come from the education system in general when these networks grow and develop into rich places for learning that are an alternative to our schools instead of a part of them.

The Learning-Network Divide in Schools

Schools have been implementing Internet technologies in varying degrees since the introduction of the web in 1994, and in many classrooms technology has come to play an important role in the delivery of the curriculum and the work that our students do. Computer-per-student ratios have consistently fallen throughout the past decade, and the digital divide—the gap between people with effective access to technology and those with limited or no access—has narrowed significantly (Gray, Thomas, & Lewis, 2010). However, we've not yet embraced the fact that in the revolution of learning on the web, access is just the first step. Take a peek inside most classrooms in most schools, and you may see interactive boards and laptops; on the surface that may look different from prior generations of classrooms. On closer inspection, though, we often see that the technologies haven't built connections with other learners from disparate parts of the world or created networks with other classrooms. We have begun to close the digital divide, but a huge "learning-network divide" remains.

The reasons for this gap are many. The biggest one is that this cultural shift has occurred with dizzying speed. At this moment, the average educator between the ages of twenty-five and sixty-five was born into a world with no world wide web, no cell phones, no smartphones, and few (if any) portable personal computers. As recently as 2000, most schools were still places where the term *technology* meant the glow of the overhead projector or the teacher's desktop computer, and for funding reasons, the physical structures of many schools still do not accommodate the tools for today's networked learning environments that we describe in this book. The revolution that began with the web in the mid-1990s has exploded with the advent of small, ubiquitously connected devices in every shape and size. The kind of technological changes that took a lifetime in previous centuries have occurred in the span of a decade, and this rate of change is accelerating, not slowing down. For an interesting perspective on the speed of this change, consider Blockbuster, which went from inception, to empire, to bankruptcy in a couple of decades (de la Merced, 2010). New communication tools such as Twitter and Facebook have risen to worldwide popularity in a few years, and the iPhone changed the ways people work and play in a matter of months. Given the breakneck pace of these changes, for many adults the phrase *virtual reality* doesn't refer to online worlds filled with avatars; it refers to the scramble to keep up in the world in which we live.

Like us, our kids experience a virtual reality, too; except theirs is when they walk into school and unplug from the networks that connect them to their world. Social media are not new or frightening or scary to kids; they are part and parcel of students' day-to-day existence. Our kids were born into a connected world, and for the vast majority of them who have access to the Internet, networking with friends online is just part of being friends—a big part, actually. A survey by Mediapost suggests that 80 percent of American teens will use social networking sites in 2011 compared to only 64 percent of all Internet users, and that almost 70 percent of all thirteen- to seventeen-year-olds will use Facebook on a weekly basis this year (McNaughton, 2011). Our children are connecting outside the school walls, using technologies that most adults are just getting used to and that most schools have not implemented. Today's kids flock to Facebook, send hundreds of text messages a day from their cell phones, and stay ubiquitously linked to their friends in ways many adults have little context for. Research is showing that their interactions in these social networks are a different yet important part of their development, shaping the way they think and see the world (Ito et al., 2008).

No question, students believe that this world should be extended into our schools. When asked to design the school of the future, "communication tools" was the number one student pick, according to Speak Up 2009, a survey of almost 300,000 K–12 students (Project Tomorrow, 2010). This was followed by "digital media," "online textbooks," "mobile computers," and "games/virtual simulations" to round out their top five. In contrast, only 27 percent of nearly 40,000 teachers surveyed thought that collaboration tools such as blogs, social networking sites, or wikis have a role in schools, and only 25 percent of future teachers responded that their preparation courses are teaching them how to use learning network tools to facilitate collaboration between students. The number-one pick of principals for the school of the future, "interactive white boards," didn't even make the student list (Project Tomorrow, 2010).

We believe that this learning-network divide between students and educators is less about philosophy and more about exposure. In our experience, the reason most educators don't see a place for these tools in schools is because many have not had the time to figure out the role these networks have in their own lives. This book aims to narrow the divide, put educators on the same footing as our kids, and provide the recipe for incorporating these tools into every classroom.

Marrying Facebook to Fantastic Learning

Just because students understand social networking and think it would be cool to use in schools doesn't mean they know how to use these tools for learning. Most students are technological consumers but not necessarily creators. We see something similar in our youngest faculty, those who grew up during the Internet age. A twenty-two-year-old teacher who shows up this year in our schools has most likely used social networks during his time in high school and college, but that doesn't mean those networks will find a meaningful use in his classroom. In the same way that learning management in college is an important but incomplete step in preparing you for a career in business, learning how to use Facebook means that you know how to network online, but it doesn't immediately translate into powerful global learning.

Students need educators to teach them to cultivate and utilize networks for learning, and this fact creates a tremendously exciting moment to be in schools. At a time when most teachers are searching for ways to meet state standards, teach complex skills, and motivate their kids, those same students are embracing the building blocks of one of the most powerful tools for learning ever invented, and most don't even know it. Furthermore, during a time when young people know much more than adults about using online networks, our industry is one of the few in which young people and adults live and work together every day with the potential of cross-pollinating adults' knowledge of learning with teenagers' knowledge of networks. To oversimplify the equation—we need educators' understanding of good pedagogy to combine with students' understanding of and enthusiasm for online networks. Our schools need to harness each student's natural propensity for participating in online spaces and funnel that energy into building powerful networks for learning that are used in every class almost every day.

Right now, this is not happening. Most educators are just starting to recognize the huge potential for learning in these online spaces—potential that can frame the way today's children will learn as they enter adulthood. For those who really understand it, the implications of this shift are overwhelming. It means that static textbooks that are outdated the day they are printed can be replaced with up-to-date information online that is continuously refreshed and renewed. It means that teachers' professional learning will take place in online connected spaces that span the globe. It means that faculty do not need to see themselves as the only conduit for teaching content and skills, but as facilitators in a worldwide network of teachers. It means that students can take more responsibility for setting and achieving individual learning goals. In short, it fulfills some of our greatest hopes for learning while challenging many of our traditional features of schooling.

Overcoming that traditional view of education is the hardest part. Embracing these tools and changing our classrooms will require letting go of preconceived notions of school, ideas we've been carrying around most of our lives. We need to see that self-learning, informal learning, and learning not connected with school are a huge part of what we need to teach. We need to go beyond tinkering on the edges of the web in which the end result does little to change the status quo. We need to grapple with the startling reality that local monopolies of learning are an artifact of the past and that the roles of our schools and our teachers are drastically different in the Internet age.

Two Problems and a Challenge

Given the powerful benefits of using these tools in their schools, why are even the most "plugged-in" educators still committed to a reform path? We admit that the field of education has a laundry list of reasons why we can't change the current model of schooling to incorporate the remarkable forms of new learning enabled by the web. (We will discuss some of these later in the book.) There are even a few among us who want to look backward instead of forward and claim that Web 2.0 technologies are just another passing educational reform—a fad that will go away like many others we have seen over the decades. There are also some who "get it" but are following the same mistake made by the newspapers, trying to take an older model of schooling and just tweak it.

But these are not the main stumbling blocks to transformation. As we talk to educators at every level of the system, they repeat two very big barriers more often than any of those mentioned previously. We have come to call these two stumbling blocks "the problems." We promise to guide you through the first if you'll take on the challenge of the second.

The Problems

More often than not, in our conversations with educators from across the country and around the world, we have come to see two main barriers to real transformation in schools. First, even though most educators will agree that real change is afoot in the world outside of education, they don't yet have enough of a grasp of what those changes mean for their schools, and if they do grasp it, it's still difficult to see a path to real implementation of those changes. Second, even though they know change is necessary, no one is asking for it.

When it comes to the first problem—lack of understanding—much of the difficulty stems from the reality that most teachers are products of this outdated system, one that they sincerely believe delivered to them an excellent education. It's what they know education to be, and it's very hard to see what a technologically rich, globally connected system might look like. Such a shift in viewpoint requires identifying the opportunities that learning networks offer our schools and then carving out a vision for a new learning landscape. That's hard work. Moreover, once this vision is in hand, it requires the creation of a step-by-step process for bringing it into every aspect of the system. Without some guidance around getting started, that's often a daunting task.

The second barrier standing in the way of change is that, frankly, no one is demanding that schools do anything differently right now. Few parents expect teachers and students to begin using social networks in teaching and learning, especially in schools with excellent reputations. Most teachers are not demanding that these tools be available in the classroom, since they are not personally using them in their own learning. School leadership is not advocating for this type of learning in the classroom, and colleges and universities are not demanding that we replace SATs and advanced placement courses with evidence that students are plugged into a global learning network. If we surveyed our students, they would probably prefer to use these tools, but they are not going to demand their use en masse in some form of modern "social networking uprising."

In addition, outside assessment systems imposed on schools are not making a clear connection between the use of these tools and student learning. State leaders and regional superintendents reviewing No Child Left Behind adequate yearly progress (AYP) results will often turn to more traditional tools to improve achievement. Individual school principals faced with poor state test results are more likely to implement after-school remediation programs that cover the same material in the same way than to incorporate a global network of teachers and change the existing classroom. Even individual teachers may not see evidence that their understanding and use of these networks is connected to their evaluation.

Finally, despite many signals that what we're doing in schools is no longer working for a growing segment of the school population—international rankings that show the United States lagging behind in the most basic of skills, employer complaints that college graduates are entering the workforce without the ability to read and write effectively, and the lack of problem-solving and critical-thinking skills by students at every level—most responses to the crisis are constrained within the traditional model of schooling (OECD, 2010). Few schools are looking to create different classrooms. Although learning networks could enable many schools to reach their individual student achievement goals, no one is clamoring for their adoption.

The Challenge

So here, in a nutshell, is our challenge: we have to find a way to do something most policymakers, educators, universities, and parents have yet to demand. We have to find ways to bring networked learning opportunities into our classrooms even while many of the traditional expectations for schools remain in place and even though the vast majority of parents still want us to prepare their children in the same way they were prepared. We have to introduce our kids to a whole new method of learning that is less about memorizing and "doing their own work" and more about content creation and collaborating with others, and doing so in the context of their passions. In other words, we have to make sure our students pass the traditional tests and can flourish in college or in the workplace while also providing them with new skills and literacies that we have not yet found a way to measure. We have to ask our teachers to learn in different ways than how they learned in their high schools and colleges in order to leverage the power of modern networks, not only for their own personal learning but to better deliver these new skills and literacies to the students in their classrooms.

No question—that will be a huge undertaking, but for the sake of our students and for our own learning, it's a challenge worth taking on sooner rather than later. We cannot wait for the Department of Education, state agencies, or local government to mandate these types of changes. The definition of *educational leader* needs to shift from the person with the title to the person with the vision. Teachers in the classroom can exercise enormous influence over the skills their students learn and the methods they use, while still delivering a state-mandated curriculum. Believe it or not, academic department heads and principals can reshape how their people learn (and therefore teach) while still meeting state test-score benchmarks. Superintendents can groom forward-looking school leaders connected to global networks of learners who expand their vision of learning. All of that is already being done in many schools around the world by teachers, administrators, and leaders who aren't waiting to be told to change, and we'll share some of their stories later in this book.

Here's the deal that we want to make with you right now. We'll help you with the first barrier, describing the vision and giving you a road map to implementation, if you are willing to embrace the challenge of the second. If you are willing to step forward and lead into the 21st century, we will show you where to go and how to get there. If you are willing to change the way that you learn, we can teach you the tools and techniques for doing it successfully. If you want to change your classroom, we will give you a recipe for doing just that. If you want to change your school, we will coach you in the best path to take. We will help you both avoid the pitfalls and succeed in the transformation, but we need you to have the courage to act even though no one is demanding it.

This is a big conversation—one that isn't for the faint of heart. For anyone who cares about kids and their future, however, it's an essential conversation that speaks directly to our responsibility as professionals to constantly improve our pedagogy and provides huge opportunities for each of us as learners ourselves.

How Can We Help?

This book is the step-by-step guide for creating globally connected schools that empower students to learn in modern ways. It takes a very challenging change process and breaks it down into components that everyone can follow. We have written this book to help both the individual educator who wants to learn differently and the administrator who is responsible for hundreds of schools.

We know that educators face the age-old problem of how to fix the hole in the boat when they are busy bailing water. Educators are busy people. The needs of students, teachers, and parents can leave little time for working out a plan to transform teaching and learning, especially when that plan needs to consider social and technological changes that evolve rapidly and continuously. With the plan we have outlined, everyday educators can use personal learning networks to effect change at every level of the school system in a relatively short period of time. Better yet, you can use the networks you create as a support system to lessen your workload and help sustain the change.

We also understand that this transformation is deeply personal. Before addressing how to create personal learning networks in schools, we want to first focus on teachers creating learning networks in their own lives. Learning something new is always challenging, but using personal learning networks for the first time is an emotional process as well as a cognitive one. Part of it involves the nuts and bolts of learning the technology, but an equally important part is putting your ideas online and interacting with people from around the globe. For this exact reason, we coach you through how to consume information as well as how to contribute, and we give you tips and pointers on how to break through some of the mental barriers that can prevent some people from fully taking advantage of this learning opportunity.

That's not to say that this change will be easy—few worthwhile changes are—but we'll try to make it as easy as possible. It's like weight loss. Everyone knows that the basic outline for losing weight is to eat less and exercise more; so why aren't more people thin? Because everyone also knows that for most people, eating less and exercising more is not easy. But what if they had help? What if a nutritionist outlined a food plan of tasty, easy-to-prepare foods? What if an exercise specialist prepared a moderate exercise plan that only took twenty minutes a day? Finally, what if a cook helped prepare the food and a partner helped with the workout? Would that make losing weight easier?

This book is like your personal nutritionist and trainer for changing your own learning, your professional practice, and your schools. Your online network will be the cook, serving up the information that you need. While these changes still won't be easy to navigate, we hope to make it easier than you expect.

What Are the Steps?

This idea of networked learning has obvious implications at many different levels, and we'll be looking at each in depth in the coming chapters. We believe there is a bottom-up progression in order to fundamentally change the way schools operate:

1. Understanding the power of PLNs

2. Becoming a networked learner

3. Implementing a networked classroom

4. Becoming a networked school

We begin by making the case for change. In chapter 1, we describe how learning is different in a globally connected world and why school models that do not embrace this change will fail our kids in the 21st century. We sketch out a vision for dynamic, connected schools in which students use modern technologies to drive their own learning not only during their time in school, but long after they have graduated.

Chapter 2 instructs you on how to create your own learning networks. In a learning context, this starts with us as individuals—not as educators, but as learners in our own right. Until you have a practical understanding of what networked learning means in your own life, it's difficult to begin meaningful conversations around what change looks like at the next levels. This process requires us to be willing to spend some time looking inward, learning to connect and interact around the things we are passionate about. We believe that if you embrace this change in your personal learning life, you will be more prepared to implement this new model of learning in your education work. Teaching about networks requires being networked; the ability to model your own use of learning networks in front of your students might be your most important pedagogy of all.

Chapter 3 discusses how to bring these changes into classrooms. Networked classrooms are the natural evolution of networked teachers. As you'll see by the stories we share in that chapter, connecting classrooms to one another for collaboration and learning is pretty easy when you yourself are connected to a network of global teachers just waiting to join their classrooms with yours. These types of connections can facilitate diversity and can be an effective way of beginning to teach your own students the literacies of interaction online.

Chapters 4 and 5 focus on transforming into a networked school. Chapter 4 shows you how to build a coherent change process for the teachers in your school or district. We'll talk about how to fashion a compelling case for change, how to pick a team to lead the change, and finally, how to roll out an extended plan to bring about these changes. In chapter 5, we provide ideas about how to bring that change to the students by finding the money, creating the support structures, defining the right policies, and overcoming the most stringent objections to integrate networked learning in all aspects of your school environment.

Our book is both theoretical and practical. It paints an inspiring picture for modern teaching and learning using world-changing technologies, but then it walks you through concrete actions to achieve that vision. It succinctly summarizes the global forces that make change an imperative for schools, and then it details the steps that can be followed by educators to change themselves, their classrooms, their schools, and their communities.

Look at this book as a road map for navigating this unique moment in the history of education, a time unlike any other from a learning standpoint. The system of education we've known for the past hundred years is changing irrevocably, and if we choose to, each of us will play a role in what happens next. To make the most of those efforts, we have to understand at a personal, professional, and community level what change really looks and feels like. We believe in your ability to do just that, and it is our sincere hope that every one of you, after reading this book, is ready for the challenge that lies ahead.

CHAPTER 1

UNDERSTANDING THE POWER OF PLNS

Pam Moran is in what she calls the "twilight" of her career in schools. Now the superintendent of the Albemarle County Schools in Virginia, home to some 1,400 educators and 13,000 students over 726 square miles, Pam has spent over thirty years in every level of education. It's been a wonderful ride without regrets, save one.

"I really wish I had another 20 years left in this career," she says. "I've spent most of my time in schools just tinkering around the edges of learning, but nothing much has really changed. But right now, things are changing at lightspeed" (P. Moran, personal communication, January 10, 2011).

For two years, Pam has been learning about learning in a different way—by connecting to other educational leaders and teachers around the world online. She's been tweeting on Twitter, gaining a following of almost three thousand readers. Her blog, *A Space for Learning* (http://spacesforlearning.wordpress .com), has quickly become a must-read for other superintendents and educators of all stripes. A quick Google search leads to many other guest blog posts, comments, and articles about her work shifting the learning environment in her district to one that is more embracing of the networks and connections that facilitate learning outside the classroom. Those experiences have transformed her view of education.

"To me, the most powerful aspect of what's happening right now is this potential for learning that we haven't even begun to appreciate yet," she says. "It's almost like we're recreating education from scratch. In another 5–10 years, education is going to look like nothing we've seen in the last 500 years. I only wish I could stick around to see it happen."

The Big Shifts

No question, we are living at a time of unprecedented change, and the web is driving much of it. As Pam suggests, the implications for learning, much less schooling, are profound. In order to fully understand those implications, we need to take a look at the fundamental shifts that are fueling our capacity to connect, interact, and learn with others in these new and different ways.

Many people have attempted to specify the ways in which the world in general is changing because of the web and the mobile technologies now exploding on the scene, but few sum it up as nicely as David Wiley, a professor of education at Brigham Young University. Wiley (2008), who is a leading thinker on the opening up of education and learning in a connected world, cites six significant shifts that are supporting connection and network building:

1. Analog to digital

2. Tethered to mobile

3. Isolated to connected

4. Generic to personal

5. Consumption to creation

6. Closed systems to open systems

These are especially relevant when trying to identify the real challenge points for K–12 schools.

First, we're moving from *analog to digital* in some very big and very fast ways. In the most obvious example, paper as a physical medium is fast giving way to the digital formats we create using technology and formats that are searchable, easier to copy and share, potentially collaborative, and more easily organized. For example, Google's attempt to scan and digitize every known book in the universe will, if successful, make those books more accessible and useful (see http://books.google.com for more information). In addition, the Stanford Engineering Library announced in 2010 that it was soon to become bookless (and journal-less) because providing that content digitally makes more sense for its students and is a precursor of what is to come in the near future. Tools like Google Docs, Evernote, and the Kindle are changing the way we interact and value paper texts in profound ways, and they are powerful signals of the information environments to come. We may not all feel comfortable living in a digital world, creating and sharing digital products, but there's no doubt the world is moving in that direction, and fast.

Second, Wiley points out that we are shifting from *tethered to mobile* technologies at an increasing pace. We no longer need to be at a desk to do our work, and in the near future we'll be able to do most of what we need to accomplish on just our phones. Apple's introduction of the iPad in 2010 has spurred a development frenzy in mid-sized touch screen tablets that can serve as an always-connected communication device and printing press to the world. More and more, people are beginning to eschew their computers for mobile devices (Hernandez, 2010). The number of people using mobile phones as their sole connection to the Internet has already grown to almost 70 percent in Egypt and near 60 percent in India (Breck, 2010). As of 2010, fully three-quarters of all U.S. teens owned cell phones (eSchool News, 2010). No question, mobile technologies pose a huge opportunity (and a huge challenge) for our classrooms.

Third, Wiley makes the point that learning is moving from being a *fundamentally isolated experience to one that is decidedly connected*. We've always had the benefit of our local connections and classrooms in which to learn, but the global connections now available have created an expectation of collaboration and cooperation around learning that goes beyond our physical space. Right now, we can be intellectually close to people who are three thousand miles away, while in the same respect, we may be far away from those sitting right next to us (P2P Foundation, 2007). In these online interactions, learning is extremely social as we read, filter, create, and share with one another on an ongoing basis.

Fourth, learning is moving from being *generic to personal*; we pursue our own interests and passions. No matter our interest, we can find others online who share that interest and with whom we can form learning groups. Take the independent school teacher from Atlanta who stood up during a professional development session and named his passion to be "mountain biking on a unicycle." Strange as it might seem, it turns out there is a whole community of "municyclists" out there who share his love of that sport. Who knew? Regardless of interest, the potential to find other like-minded souls with whom to learn makes our own learning much more self-directed, on demand, and individualized.

Fifth, as mentioned previously, this new world is all about *creation, not consumption*. Certainly, we continue to spend a large amount of our learning time reading, thinking, and synthesizing ideas. Now, however, we don't just consume those ideas; we share them. As Clay Shirky suggests in *Cognitive Surplus* (2010), we are in the process of taking the roughly two hundred billion collective hours per year we spend in front of the television set (in the U.S. alone) and turning them into creative acts, some more foolish and inane than others, but creative nonetheless. We are beginning to participate in some amazing ways:

> When someone buys a TV, the number of consumers goes up by one, but the number of producers stays the same. On the other hand, when someone buys a computer or a mobile phone, the number of consumers and producers both increase by one. Talent remains unequally distributed, but the raw ability to make and to share is now widely distributed and getting wider every year . . . Conversations among groups can now be carried out in the same media environments as broadcasts. This new option bridges the two older options of broadcast and communications media. All media can now slide from one to the other. A book can stimulate public discussion in a thousand places at once. An e-mail conversation can be published by its participants. An essay intended for public consumption can anchor a private argument, parts of which

become public. We move from public to private and back again in ways
that weren't possible in an era when public and private media, like the
radio and the telephone, used different devices and different networks.
(Shirky, 2010, Kindle location 739)

Finally, Wiley offers up a sixth shift, one that might be most challenging of all when it comes to education. In just about every area of life, we are moving from *closed systems and ideas to open ones*. Most of us know the story of open source software, programs that are created by passionate coders improving on work that is freely accessible online. Programs like the Firefox browser and Apache server software have become integral to the way we use the web. Now, however, open content is becoming more ubiquitous; it is content created without copyright restrictions, freely published and shared, and available for others to use and reuse. Examples like MIT Open-CourseWare (http://ocw.mit.edu), which provides materials from every one of MIT's two thousand courses free online, or Flat World Knowledge (www.flatworldknowledge.com), which allows textbook authors to write and freely distribute work online, are only a small slice of what is happening. We have the chance to do what Shirky calls "planet scale sharing" (Shirky, 2010, Kindle location 2302), and it's becoming an expectation that we do just that with the information we find, create, and learn.

Rethinking Learning

All of these shifts have huge implications for us as educators. In fact, even those of us living at the heart of these changes feel some discomfort trying to think through all the ways the web challenges the traditional structures of schools, classrooms, and learning. But here's the thing: given these opportunities for connection that the web now brings us, we are convinced that schools will start leveraging the power of these networks. Here are the two game-changing conditions that make that statement hard to deny: if we have access to the Internet, (1) we now have two billion potential teachers, and soon, (2) the sum of human knowledge will be at our fingertips.

That, in no uncertain terms, is different.

Most schools were built on the idea that knowledge and teachers are scarce. When you have limited access to information and you want to deliver what you do have to every citizen in an era with little communication technology, you build what schools are today: age-grouped, discipline-separated classrooms run by an expert adult who can manage the successful completion of the curriculum by a hundred or so students at a time. We mete out that knowledge in discrete parts, carefully monitoring our students' progress through one-size-fits-all assessments, deeming them "educated" when they have proven their mastery at, more often than not, getting the right answer and, to a lesser degree, displaying certain skills that show a literacy in reading and writing. Most of us know these systems intimately. And for 120 years or so, they've pretty much delivered what we've asked them to.

But what happens when knowledge and teachers aren't scarce? What happens when it's easy to connect our passion to learn to the resources to learn it? What happens when, in the next decade or so, almost everyone gains access to these profoundly different learning spaces filled with teachers and content through the devices they carry in their pockets? What happens when we don't need schools to manage the delivery of content anymore, when we can get it on our own, anytime we need it, from anywhere we're connected, from anyone who might be connected with us? Things change.

For each of us as learners, the fundamental change is that we can be much more in control of the learning we do. It's not about the next unit in the curriculum as much as it is about what we need to know when we need to know it. It's not even about what we carry around in our heads— all of that "just in case" knowledge that schools are so good at making sure students get these days. As Jay Cross, the author of *Informal Learning*, suggests, in a connected world, it's more about how much knowledge you can access with your personal learning network. "'What can you do?' has been replaced with, 'What can you and your network connections do?' Knowledge itself is moving from the individual to the individual and his contacts" (Cross, 2006, p. 18). If we have access to our networks, we're a lot smarter than we used to be. In fact, "connection with others in a network is of prime importance in having access to a wide repository of knowledge," according to Vance Stevens of the Petroleum Institute in Abu Dhabi (Stevens, 2009). In other words, if we want to make the most of our brains these days, we need to connect online.

What hasn't changed is this: learning, online or off, is still social, and that's good news for all of us. If you think we're sketching a vision of students sitting in front of computers working through self-paced curricula and interacting with a teacher only on occasion, you're way, way off. That's not what we think of as effective online learning. What we are suggesting, however, is that because of the connections we can now make on the web, there is as much potential (if not more) for meaningful, experiential, constructivist learning to occur in the interactions between people online as there is in face-to-face interactions. That's not to say that face-to-face learning isn't important or valuable. It is. But so is the web. It's the melding of the two that will shape our schools in the 21st century.

It's Not as Easy as It Looks

While participating in these online spaces may appear easy, creating a PLN is in fact a highly complex intellectual and emotional task. How do we sift through the oceans of information online to find the most relevant, trustworthy content for our studies? How do we find, vet, connect, and learn with all of those great potential teachers? How do we develop the attention skills we need in order to learn effectively and the reflection skills to assess our progress toward our learning goals? That's hard work.

Yet such participation is also exactly why we need schools to transform the role they now play in our children's lives. In other words, in this "anytime, anywhere, anyone" learning world, how do schools help students become skilled at taking charge of their own learning as well? How do we help them take full advantage of the plethora of teachers and content available to them without drowning in it? We're not suggesting we just give them all a computer and access and let them run amok online. What we are suggesting is that we give them all a computer and access and teach them how to learn effectively in this always-on, global classroom that each of them can fashion for herself or himself. This type of learning includes how to make connections with others online, how to negotiate the interactions between them, how to collaborate with them in ways that go beyond just sharing existing information to the creation of new knowledge, and how to perhaps even change the world. That attitude shift is captured in one of our favorite quotes by the philosopher Eric Hoffer: "In times of change, learners inherit the earth, while the learned find themselves beautifully equipped to deal with a world that no longer exists" (Hoffer, n.d.).

Schools have been working hard at making our kids *learned* because in the past, it was hard for them to do that without the teachers and resources that schools offered. Not so today. In the 21st century, students inhabit a world in which we have the ability to truly make them *learners* who are able to create and share and participate in these online spaces in ways that will allow them to take advantage of whatever opportunities currently exist and the unimaginable ones that lie just around the corner. To do that, we adults in the room need to be learners in those contexts as well. (More about that in the next chapter.)

Please hear this loud and clear: we're not talking about getting rid of schools. We are, however, talking about seriously rethinking the way they work to meet the needs of the current learning realities our students face. While knowledge and information may now more and more reside outside the four walls, we as educators still can and *should* be the learning experts in our students' lives. Schools are part of a larger PLN. Therefore, this is not the end of schools and teachers as much as it is the dawn of a new age of schooling, one that is much more relevant to students and learners of all stripes. It's a daunting moment, for sure, but it's also one that we think is filled with opportunity for all of us.

So at this moment, we are left with two vastly different snapshots of what learning looks like inside and outside of schools. One is a black-and-white photo that depicts a student sitting at her desk alone, studying from a mass-produced book, preparing a paper assessment for a classroom teacher who periodically assesses her learning, and waiting to take the culminating assessment that stamps her as being "educated." The second, meanwhile, is a full-color video of that same student learning from a local teacher how to interact with personalized content accessed through a mobile device, sharing her thoughts with dozens of teachers from around the world, and receiving real-time feedback on the written and multimedia contributions that she offers. A bit of a contrast, wouldn't you say? And yes, we know that full-color video isn't playing in every classroom across this country or the world. We have a lot of work to do to get kids connected and to teach them how to learn well in these networked spaces, but there's no longer any doubt that we are quickly moving in that direction. Education has little time to waste to move there as well. Only by fully understanding the power of learning networks can we clearly decide which image we want for our schools.

Stephen Downes, a senior researcher for Canada's National Research Council, does a great job of summing up these big shifts in a compelling essay titled "A World to Change" at the *Huffington Post*:

> We need, first, to take charge of our own learning, and next, help others take charge of their own learning. We need to move beyond the idea that an education is something that is provided for us, and toward the idea that *an education is something that we create for ourselves*. It is time, in other words, that we change our attitude toward learning and the educational system in general. (Downes, 2010, emphasis added)

We couldn't agree more.

Learning Networks

So what exactly do we mean when we say "learning networks"? We mean the rich set of connections each of us can make to people in both our online and offline worlds who can help us with our learning pursuits. While we've always had those types of people in our day-to-day lives, the Internet pushes the potential scope and scale of those networks to unprecedented heights. Today we can turn to all sorts of professionals and collaborators from anywhere in the world to help us answer our questions, connect us to relevant content and resources, or just share their own experiences with us. While these connections are surely social in nature, we think they go beyond the popular "social network" moniker that has been applied to Facebook, MySpace, and others. For the most part, in those spaces, we connect to people we already know and love, friends, or friends of friends. Learning networks are very different both in form and purpose in that we instead connect with people we don't already know—helpful strangers who share our passion for a particular topic. We make those connections not just to keep in touch—we make them to learn. In these new learning spaces, we share links using tools like Twitter or Edmodo, offer up our thoughts on one another's blogs, act as critical friends, push one another's thinking, and collaboratively create new knowledge to share with the world. These are primarily intellectual exercises, not social ones. In fact, while our interactions with these strangers can in many cases become friendly, it's not uncommon to keep these learning and social spaces very separate.

Simply put, online learning networks change the game by allowing us, in a sense, to create our own global classrooms and collect teachers and other learners around the topics we want to learn about. They allow us to self-direct our learning in exciting new ways, ways in which schools are going to find it increasingly hard to compete with. As authors Tony Bingham and Marcia Conner write, networks "provide people at every level, in every nook of the organization and every corner of the globe, a way to reclaim their natural capacity to learn non-stop" (2010, Kindle location 319).

Many of our students are starting to do this. The 2008 MacArthur Foundation report *Living and Learning With New Media* found that students certainly use the web in friendship-based ways by staying connected to the people they know in their face-to-face worlds. But they also use the web to connect in interest-based ways, which, as the name suggests, is all about their passions to learn; whether it's fixing up that '78 Camaro, finding ways to clean up the environment, or learning how to build an awesome new skateboard, kids are beginning to engage in these networked online spaces on their own. As the lead author of the study, Mimi Ito writes, "Kids learn on the Internet in a self-directed way, by looking around for information they are interested in, or connecting with others who can help them. This is a big departure from how they are asked to learn in most schools" (Ito et al., 2008).

That type of learning *is* a big departure, and it's one that we have to understand for ourselves if we are to make sense of what roles schools and classrooms are going to play in this much more self-directed learning world. This is not the linear, one-size-fits-all, all-in-one-place learning system. In these online spaces, content and knowledge are much more decentralized and distributed, are found in many places instead of one, and are also much more individualized. As our students come to expect these customized, highly personalized learning interactions online more and more, our systems' inability to provide the same type of experience in the classroom will no doubt continue to challenge the relevance of school in their eyes.

We think this shift is a huge opportunity, however. Schools can do more than remain relevant; they can become even more important in our students' lives, if we are willing to deeply rethink our role in these contexts. Again, we're not suggesting this will happen overnight. We are suggesting, however, that every school system has to begin to move in these directions, toward enabling every student to self-direct his or her own learning and make sense of the complexities and opportunities that all of us now face. It's a huge task.

It all starts with understanding deeply how these learning networks work. George Siemens, a professor at Athabasca University in Edmonton, Calgary, and a leading thinker about these shifts, suggests that our connections to one another and to relevant content in a global context are absolutely essential to becoming educated these days. These passion-based connections help us filter through the incredible amount of information the web holds today, and within these networks, we now are creating knowledge together, testing theories and ideas, collaborating on solutions or actions, and sharing back most everything we learn in the process. It's a highly transparent process that, while uncomfortable for many adults, is more and more the expectation for our students and their learning.

Today, according to Siemens (2007), "learning is a network formation process of connecting specialized nodes or information sources." It is not about memorizing facts. He argues, much like Jay Cross, that knowledge actually resides in these networks, and that an integral part of the learning process is to be able find and synthesize the most current information and recognize connections between ideas that may be found in many different places from many different people. Since learning is an ongoing process and no longer an event, our ability to expand our knowledge is more important than we currently realize (Siemens, 2007).

We see this process of connecting playing out all around us online all the time. Through our interactions with the people and resources in our networks, we become a part of an ongoing flow of learning. Every day there is new knowledge to make sense of and new ways of thinking about and looking at the world. As we participate in these spaces, we become one node, one participant of many in a network that in aggregate is constantly learning. In other words, even though we may not be connected at a given moment, invariably others in our network are, and they are reading, filtering, thinking, and sharing in transparent ways that will be available to us when we do go back online.

New Literacies

To participate fully in this new learning environment, our students will need a host of new skills and literacies, as will we. The situation begs the question of all of us: "At a moment of so many shifts, am I literate?" Lots of folks are starting to ask that question, and some of them—like the National Council of Teachers of English (NCTE), the International Society for Technology in Education (ISTE), and even the federal government—are bringing some important weight to the conversation.

We suggest that the focus of any conversations around new skills should center on this defining question: how do we best begin to create, navigate, and grow our own learning networks in safe, effective, and ethical ways? The answer to that question is highly complex, but we think it starts with a combination of old and new skills and literacies. While many are touting the idea of 21st century skills, most are really 19th century skills that are being reframed in important ways for learning in these networked spaces.

NCTE has created a useful definition of what literate readers and writers should be able to do considering the changes in information and content production. As the organization suggests, "These literacies—from reading online newspapers to participating in virtual classrooms—are multiple, dynamic, and malleable" (NCTE, 2008). What is defined as literate today may not suffice tomorrow, given the fast-paced changes in technology. As you read through these measures of literacy, try to apply them to your own practice. Be honest, because your literacy in these six contexts is crucial to the lens you bring to the larger conversation around change:

1. Developing proficiency with the tools of technology

2. Building relationships with others to pose and solve problems collaboratively and cross-culturally

3. Designing and sharing information for global communities to meet a variety of purposes

4. Managing, analyzing, and synthesizing multiple streams of simultaneous information

5. Creating, critiquing, analyzing, and evaluating multimedia texts

6. Attending to the ethical responsibilities required by these complex environments

Odds are you're not feeling very literate at the moment. While more and more teachers are exhibiting proficiency at using technology, a very small percentage of educators are actually solving problems with partners from other cultures, creating and sharing information with the world, and producing—much less deconstructing—multimedia texts. These are all expectations of literacy that, for the most part, weren't in place when we came through the school systems ourselves. But there is no question that the list captures much of what today's social learning online requires.

Although it's not specifically articulated by NCTE, there is also a larger expectation here, namely that technology, primarily the web, is simply a seamless part of how we conduct our business in schools today. Not one of those measures (aside from perhaps the last) can be accomplished without some type of computer—whether it be a desktop, laptop, tablet, or cell phone—and a connection. Most of them can happen on any of those devices. Seamless access is not a state that we have achieved in most of our schools. It's a challenge that still lies ahead.

ISTE has taken the step to define these new skills and literacies separately for students, teachers, and administrators. For instance, the most recent group of standards, written for administrators in 2009, expects school leaders to "promote and participate in local, national, and global learning communities that stimulate innovation, creativity, and digital-age collaboration" (ISTE, 2009). We expect similar language to appear in the student and teacher standards in the next edition.

Similarly, the current *National Education Technology Plan 2010* provides some compelling language to guide our thinking about change. First, it calls for "a revolutionary transformation rather than an evolutionary tinkering" of the education system (United States Department of Education, 2010a). It advocates "personalized learning instead of a one-size-fits-all curriculum," and it calls for every student and every teacher to have an Internet-connected device. We find what they do with those devices compelling. In the "Teaching: Prepare and Connect" section, the plan states that "social networks can be used to provide educators with career-long personal learning tools and resources that make professional learning timely and relevant as well as an ongoing activity that continually improves practice and evolves their skills over time." It mentions online communities of learners and "anytime, anywhere" learning as well. (We feel compelled to note, however, that for all of the forward-thinking rhetoric offered by the plan, there is no real indication of how these ideas square with the much more traditional view of the "Race to the Top" initiative that is the centerpiece of the current educational vision.)

Finally, we'll point to the findings of the *2010 Horizon Report*, a widely respected annual compilation of education and technology issues created by a thirty-five-member panel of thought leaders in the field. The report states that because "the abundance of resources and relationships made easily accessible via the Internet is increasingly challenging us to revisit our roles as educators in sense-making, coaching, and credentialing . . . the role of the academy—and the way we prepare students for their future lives—is changing" (Johnson, Levine, Smith, & Stone, 2010, pp. 3–4). The authors articulate the many challenges and opportunities that schools face at the moment, all of which revolve around the critical connections we can now make online.

In one way or another, all of these organizations, and many others, are articulating a very simple idea: there is now an easy connection between a person's passion to learn something and the resources to learn it. It's called a network, and it needs to be a part of any literate adult or student life. Our connections ease the path to technology proficiency, problem solving, and accessing and sharing information widely. They help us do the hard work of making sense of information, and in many ways, they keep us on track in terms of how we use these tools in our lives. In other words, in order for our students to become "literate" as defined by NCTE, technology will have to become a part of our learning culture. Just like paper and pen, a device and a connection are required tools for our learning trade now, and we have to begin to change our culture to not only embrace these shifts but take full advantage of the potentials they create, which means each of us working to make the web an integral part of our learning practices.

Changing Skills

Integrating the web into our learning practices also means changing the way we learn and work as schools. For instance, as we build and begin to participate in our networks, we must be constantly assessing both the content we view and the people we meet, as opposed to having the traditional teacher vet those types of interactions. You can believe the textbook. You can trust the teacher. When texts and teachers are all over the place, however, it becomes crucial that learners of all ages be able to answer the questions "What can I believe?" and "Who can I trust?" during every interaction online. Networked learners consistently pose these two questions as they navigate their interactions.

Similarly, in an online environment fraught with so many potential distractions, how do we teach ourselves and our students to maintain a level of attention and focus that will allow them to learn deeply? Take, for instance, the idea of "continuous partial attention," a term coined by Linda Stone to describe our desire not to miss anything on the web. It's common to be writing a blog post (or a book) while having the latest Twitter or Facebook post pop-up, getting an email alert, or finding a hundred other ways to participate in the moment. That may be one way of parceling out our attention at any given moment, one "attention strategy," as Stone (2010) puts it, but it's one that many find habit forming. Others, such as authors Nicholas Carr (2010, *The Shallows*) and Mark Bauerlein (2008, *The Dumbest Generation*) have argued with some effect that all of the potential distractions that the web creates can have a negative effect on memory and deep thinking. We don't disagree that there are potential downsides that we have yet to begin to understand.

But we also feel that these are challenges that can and, frankly, must be addressed through education and the cultivation of healthy practice, not by cutting back access. For instance, we agree with author and educator Howard Rheingold who has been exploring the idea of an "attention literacy" that is crucial to navigating these networks well. He writes:

> Attention is a skill that must be learned, shaped, practiced; this skill must evolve if we are to evolve. The technological extension of our minds and brains by chips and nets has granted great power to billions of people, but even in the early years of always-on, it is clear to even technology enthusiasts like me that this power will certainly mislead, mesmerize and distract those who haven't learned—were never taught—how to exert some degree of mental control over our use of laptop, handheld, ear-budded media. (Rheingold, 2009)

This poses a huge challenge for both individuals and the systems they work in, one that we'll dive into more deeply in later chapters.

In the end, these types of skills must become a seamless and integral part of how we interact with information and people online, and as educators, we have to be able to model these for our students. The reality is that networks themselves help answer these questions routinely. If you have the ability to grow your connections by choosing trustworthy and believable people to interact with in the first place, that network can help you edit and vet the new connections you make.

Network Effects

So what would our schools look like if everyone from state leaders to classroom teachers embraced learning networks? Well, frankly, each school would probably look exciting but unique. Learning networks are not a one-size-fits-all solution that works for each school in the same way. Quite the contrary, one of the reasons these tools are so powerful is their ability to serve a variety of goals. In this way, they are unlike a national or state curriculum or some of the reform initiatives that structure classroom instruction in very specific ways. You can personalize your use of these networks to meet your local goals.

Yet schools using these networks do have some things in common that result from the transformational power of these tools. Whether your language classes are talking to students in South America, your English students are blogging with the author of the novel they're reading, or your science classes are creating a video with scientists from the National Institute of Health, schools immersed in global learning networks share at least seven common traits:

1. Students are better prepared for life and work in the 21st century.

2. Classrooms are more engaging.

3. Students are responsible for their own learning.

4. Instruction is more individualized.

5. Adults become better at their jobs and build problem-solving capacity.

6. Students are safer.

7. Schools save time and money.

First, students are better prepared for life and work in the 21st century. Participation in learning networks gives them the opportunity to practice the "seven survival skills," defined by Harvard education professor Tony Wagner in *The Global Achievement Gap* as (1) critical thinking/problem solving, (2) accessing and analyzing information, (3) collaboration/leading by influence, (4) agility and adaptability, (5) initiative and entrepreneurialism, (6) effective oral and written communication, and finally, (7) curiosity and imagination (Wagner, 2010). As part of learning how to build these networks, students learn invaluable media literacy skills that reinforce their ability to think critically about Internet information and access the most up-to-date information quickly and efficiently. Online exchanges have the potential to raise their oral and written communication skills; students writing about topics they are passionate about for a real audience will improve their writing level. The teachers and students with whom they interact in these networks increase the diversity of their ideas and make them better prepared to collaborate globally to answer local questions. Learning networks serve as a gateway to learning many of the skills students will need in life and work. As e-learning specialist Ellen Wagner says, "Today we assess personal mastery of knowledge and skills with how well people can leverage their interconnected networks of connections to resources, information, and subject matter specialists. Workplace success has shifted from individual accomplishment to teams, communities of practice, and collaboration" (as cited in Bingham & Conner, 2010, Kindle location 654).

Second, classrooms are more engaging. These networks give our students and teachers the opportunity to learn from people across the globe. For students, this means being able to approach challenges from a different angle, accessing information and teachers that can enhance their understanding and meet their personal needs. For teachers, these same networks can connect them to discussions about engaging content, well-designed assessments, and effective instructional strategies. Classrooms become intersections for people and ideas as they are filled with a flow of information and conversation from around the world.

Third, students are responsible for their own learning. Students learn how to learn in the Internet age by building their own networks and managing them over time. Students can build these networks to meet the expectations of the local curriculum and to learn about their interests outside of school. By interfacing with experts from around the world, students can approach the curriculum from different angles and with different teachers, and they have the opportunity to receive real feedback on real issues, feedback that increases the frequency and the diversity in their assessments. Furthermore, they take with them the skills they need to be lifelong learners, using those skills in schooling, work, and personal endeavors.

Fourth, instruction is more individualized. Students who participate in these networks begin by sharing resources from around the world, but over time they personalize their networks with the information and people that help them the most. This means that instead of a generic textbook, students cultivate a text filled with resources that fit their learning style. This approach works when working on the state curriculum or simply pursuing their personal passions.

Fifth, the connections created in personal learning networks can help every adult in the school system become better at his or her job and can build capacity in a school to developing solutions to difficult challenges. In a school that embraces learning networks, adults are actively learning all the time, enriching both their theoretical understanding of their profession and their practical day-to-day work. This kind of learning offers the opportunity to get feedback on potential solutions, and it raises school performance and student achievement by giving daily access to tested solutions from peers in the field. Furthermore, since these networks reach beyond the local community, adults in the school have their work informed by ideas and practices from educators (and non-educators) from around the world. When schools are communities of active learners, every student benefits.

Sixth, students are safer. Kids in the lowest grades of our school systems have access to Internet connections on their computers, toys, games, and mobile devices. As much as we might wish that we could monitor their behavior all the time, the reality is that students will most likely be online doing things without our knowledge. In schools with instruction on learning networks, one of the first things students are taught is how to be safe online. Students learn how to limit the sharing of personal information and how to craft an age-appropriate personal profile that will not embarrass them later in life. They learn what kind of content is appropriate to share online in a moral, legal, and ethical sense. Students learn how to form appropriate relationships online that benefit their learning. These actions teach students how to navigate the powerful yet tricky waters of the Internet in safe, ethical, and productive ways.

Seventh, schools save time and money. Everyone knows that one-shot professional development is expensive and ineffective. It is difficult to learn something in a single day (or a few days) and successfully apply it without receiving reinforcement or support. Instead, learning networks substitute free resources from around the world and then embed a support system for implementing the work. Most importantly, teachers take ownership of their own professional development, seeking out the resources and people who can help them learn new tools, revise lesson plans, connect with other learners, and much more. Professional learning becomes an ongoing, job-embedded process, one not dependent on in-service days or prep periods. Schools that use these tools also expand their time for professional development, since these networks become a part of teachers' regular practice all year.

These seven benefits are available to every type of school that embraces this shift toward a more globally networked learning culture for students and teachers—public or private, charter or for-profit. We won't lie to you; this isn't an easy shift to make. It takes vision, planning, communication, and commitment to move to a networked learning culture. But if you do make the shift, rest assured that these approaches will work with any curriculum—state mandated, locally developed, or somewhere in between. They are implementable at any grade level, from students who are about to graduate all the way down to the smallest learners who just arrived in our schools. They can help prepare students for rigorous state assessments, can help schools make adequate yearly progress, and can meet the learning goals of individual students and teachers. The networks bring the world to your doorstep, whether that door is in a small town with a few hundred people or the busy streets of downtown Manhattan.

Let's also be clear that this shift is not about the gadgets and the tech toys. It's not about whether your classroom has an interactive whiteboard or whether your district has purchased the most recent tablet computer. To use an analogy coined by technology journalist Matt Richtel, "some technology is Twinkies and some technology is Brussels sprouts" (NPR, 2010). Certain tools are important to leverage the power of new learning, but the most important tools for the modern schools are the teachers and administrators who learn by accessing a global network themselves.

There are very few prerequisites for your school to undertake this remarkable transformation—computers connected to the Internet and a willingness to expand the boundaries and structure of the traditional classroom. Each school will use these networks in different ways, and everyone will benefit from a more engaged, more diverse, and safer community of active learners who are ready for life and work in the 21st century.

Does It Work?

Our online networks are filled with thousands of educators who will speak to the positive effects of learning networks on student achievement and especially on student engagement. By having students connect with real people outside the classroom, the teachers we've spoken with report students learning more deeply and with more engagement than a standard in-class approach focused on textbooks and handouts.

For schools that are measured by standardized test scores and state tests, it's natural to ask for research that supports the connection between the use of PLNs in the classroom and improved learning in the traditional sense. Because of the still relative newness of the web and the somewhat limited adoption of these technologies in classrooms to date, however, that research is hard to find in any quantitative form. The research situation is clouded by at least two other factors. First, as we suggested in the opening, these new social technologies and networks open up a whole new world of important learning, one that is difficult to adequately measure on traditional assessments. In short, PLNs require skills and literacies that are difficult to tie to "student achievement" as it is currently being defined. Second, the vast majority of teachers haven't had the experience of learning in these networks for themselves, and therefore they haven't yet come to understand the real opportunities of these connected classrooms for student learning. (We'll focus on those issues much more deeply in chapters 2 and 3.)

Here is some of the initial research that has been published about learning online. In 2009, a Department of Education meta-analysis concluded that online learning was actually more effective than classroom learning—primarily because of the potentials for collaboration—and that blended approaches actually were most effective of all (United States Department of Education, 2010c). While the study did not specifically look at the personal, self-directed learning networks that we are advocating here, it lends some hefty support to the potentials of the web as an effective and important learning environment. Similarly, a 2010 study by Edvantia looked at the student achievement of West Virginia students involved in Globaloria, a social learning network created in 2006 for web-based game design and simulation practice (Chadwick & Gore, 2010). Researchers found that students involved in the study significantly improved their performance on social studies and science assessments.

The key here is the focus on collaboration. Learning networks are one of the richest ways for students to collaborate online, whether it is with a student in their class or a teacher halfway around the world. If you need research study results to justify your use of the tools in your school, the literature on collaboration will be your staunchest ally.

Looking Forward Versus Looking Backward

So all of this presents us with an interesting choice in terms of how we as educators think of those trillion-plus pages of content and two billion people connections "out there." A few will choose to look at that reality and see a threat, a world filled with bogus information or strangers who perhaps mean our students harm. They block and filter and choose not to support any potential connections made by kids online. Some see it as irrelevant, just a change in society that has little to do with learning. Perhaps they add a unit on information literacy or Internet safety in an attempt to cover these new challenges. For the most part, they react like the newspapers, unwilling to wrestle with the implications of these breakthroughs. In our travels, we've seen not only social networking sites like Facebook and MySpace or collaborative sites like Wikipedia blocked; some schools even filter the major search engines like Google and Bing. "Keeping kids safe" is usually the main reason given for putting so much of the Internet at bay, but we suspect that it has much to do with being an easy way not to have to deal with the real-world realities that the web brings, good or bad.

We do believe, however, that the majority of educators, when given the facts, will embrace this moment; our students have so much knowledge and so many teachers from around the globe with whom they can learn and create. The truth about the world right now is that if we have the access and the skills to do it well, we can connect with far smarter, more learned, more passionate people online than we can find in our own physical spaces, and we can get much better, more current, more diverse information online than what we find in traditional texts. This process is filled with complexity and nuance, but we see that as a wonderful opportunity, provided we have prepared our students well enough to create and navigate those connections in safe, effective, and ethical ways. We also understand what a huge shift in thinking is required for individuals, classrooms, schools, and systems to fully take advantage of this opportunity.

To many of us, these shifts all feel daunting, too big, too much to make sense of, and too complex. Regardless of how it feels, it begs the question: what about education changes now? In this new learning world, one where content and teachers are everywhere, where passion and participation rule the day, mustn't one of our central roles become teaching our students to create their own learning groups (and networks and communities), to find and talk to strangers online with whom they share an interest so they can continue to learn without us?

These are hard questions, ones not easily answered by the addition of the new "gadget du jour." They require a deep understanding of the complex changes that are happening right now, and they also require a willingness to re-examine every aspect of our profession in that light. They require a commitment to do what's best for our children, to prepare them for their future regardless of the pressures coming from the state, from parents, and from the community. In short, as much as we may feel a deep connection to and a comfort with the structures, systems, and traditions of the schools where we ourselves were educated, we have to see the world for what it is, not what it was.

For our kids' sake, we don't have much choice.

CHAPTER 2

BECOMING A NETWORKED LEARNER

There is no single moment that Tony Baldasaro can remember that made him realize he needed to radically change the way he thought about learning. But for the assistant superintendent of the Exeter, New Hampshire, school district, the 2009–2010 school year proved to be a transformative experience when it came to his own learning, the way he thought about student learning, and his role as a leader for his teachers.

A New Way to Look at Learning

"I was a competent yet introverted school leader," Tony recalls. He was willing to share his feelings about education with his close circle of friends but was uncomfortable making them known too widely. Over the course of that school year, however, things changed dramatically. "I became what I would call a transparent leader," he says, a shift that he describes as "the most transformational event of my professional life" (T. Baldasaro, personal communication, August 13, 2010).

For Tony, that "event" centered on the online global learning networks and communities he chose to become a part of that year, networks that in just a short time gave him a voice and a perspective on education that he could not have imagined a year earlier. While no one reason drove him to learning networks, he did attend a three-day workshop on the topic and "couldn't turn back." He started a blog called *TransLeadership* (http://transleadership .wordpress.com/) where he wrote and reflected regularly on his role as a school leader. He became active on Twitter (@baldy7) and started following and participating with other educational leaders from around the world, people who pushed his thinking and deepened his learning around the changing landscape of education each step of the way. Before long, he had literally hundreds of connections willing to share their ideas, provide feedback, give advice, and on occasion, meet up for dinner. In short, this marked the beginning of his personal learning network, which now consists of the people and resources who contribute to his do-it-yourself professional development (DIYPD, as some call it) whenever he is connected to the Internet.

"I'm still humbled by the readership of my blog and the number of people who follow me on Twitter," Tony says. "These are people who now provide a tremendous amount of value to my life, people who impact me on a daily basis. The willingness of the community to welcome me to the conversation has been remarkable."

The Path to Learning Networks

Tony's introduction to a networked learning life is no longer unusual. Each day, hundreds if not thousands of educators around the world take that first step to connecting online, to share ideas about the profession with other educators or to connect with other learners looking to deepen their knowledge around a particular topic—everything from cooking to politics to passions as unique as mountain biking on a unicycle. But Tony's story departs from many others regarding the speed and scale at which his network has grown. Within a year, he had found not only a group of willing, passionate educators to interact with, but he had also found his voice in the conversation. Both have led to what he calls "amazing learning." But here is the thing: you don't have to be like Tony to experience some amazing learning on your own. There is a path for every person into this networked learning space, and all that is required to make good use of it is a willingness to participate.

And participate we must, if we are to fully understand the implications of these shifts at the curriculum, classroom, school, or systems level. It's not enough to employ these tools and technologies with our students; we have to employ them in our own learning practice. Otherwise, nothing changes. The vast majority of classroom uses of blogs, for example, are little more than taking what has already been done on paper for eons and publishing it in a different medium. In these cases, nothing has changed because the person at the front of the room (or in the front office) doesn't understand that a blog is not simply about publishing; it's about connecting. The great opportunity these tools provide is that they allow us to interact with others out there, but it's an opportunity that's meaningful only if we experience the full potential that exists in those interactions.

As we move through this book to take a closer look at how we can begin to change our classrooms, our schools, and ultimately our districts and communities, remember that *it all begins with your individual practice*. These changes require a fundamental understanding of how learning networks work in your own practice. As Tony suggests, it's difficult not to look at school practices in a different light once you've been immersed in these very different learning spaces. Those five billion people who will be on the Internet in 2020 are our potential teachers as well as our students (richhoward, 2010). It's hard to deny that this growth in numbers of users represents an amazing chance for all of us to be connected to a global community of learners. Most importantly, it also leaves little doubt that the learning future for our students resides in these networked spaces as well.

Guideposts for Learning in Networks

Before we take a look at some of the specific ways to begin making these connections and building these networks, we'll clarify what networked learning environments and interactions look like by discussing the following:

- Passion to learn

- Sharing

- Quality, not quantity

- Well-developed sense of self-direction

- Balance

- Reflection

- Face-to-face networks

Learning in networks begins with our *passion to learn*, whatever the topic. Just because you are an educator doesn't mean you have to start by building your network around the subject you teach. The great news about being online today is that it doesn't matter what your passion is, someone else out there shares it. Whether it's making stained glass or the Liverpool soccer team, finding that person, making a connection, and learning with her may do more to inform your ability to eventually help your students along their own paths than just staying within the area of your classroom expertise. In many ways, what we learn about how to interact with others online is just as important as what we learn about the topic at hand.

Those connections start with *sharing*, which is the lifeblood of networked learning. Just as we seek those who add value to our learning lives, succeeding in these networked spaces requires that we give back as much if not more than we receive. Whether it's posting a great link on Twitter, saving a bookmark to Diigo, or publishing a video of a presentation at your school (all of which we'll talk about in more depth in a moment), the easiest way to enhance your own networked learning experience is to share as much of the valuable stuff you learn as often as you can. To whatever extent you are comfortable, these learning networks require a bit of our personal selves as well. It may mean a tweet or two about your vacation, posting a favorite recipe, or some other rich detail of your life, simply to remind us of your human face. Regardless, as Brigham Young professor David Wiley (2008) says, "Without sharing, there is no education." We couldn't agree more.

Once we do start connecting, it's all about the *quality of the connections you make, not the quantity*. This idea pertains to choosing connections carefully as well as choosing diverse connections. While we have always needed to be skilled at identifying relevance in our learning interactions, with the literally billions of potential sources at our disposal right now, it's imperative that we find those that offer the most return for our time investment. That's not to say scale is a bad thing; there is much to be said for the "strength of weak ties" upon which most of our network interactions will be built, but a natural outgrowth of any social space is that some of those "nodes" will become more important than others. Managing the ratio of signal to noise in your learning flow is, as NCTE (2008) suggests, a crucial part of literacy at the moment, so choose those nodes well. Since humans have a herd mentality to begin with, it's easy to want to network with like-minded others. Diversity, however, is a key factor in taking full advantage of networked learning. To some extent, quality in networks requires us to seek those who respectfully disagree and make them a part of our online classrooms as well.

Using networks well requires a *well-developed sense of self-direction*. Networked learning is not linear. There are few if any texts, syllabi, assignments, or deadlines. The people, conversations, and content that you'll be immersing yourself in are distributed all over the web, glued together with the judicious use of links by the people you connect with. This may be, in fact, the most difficult shift to get used to in terms of the contrast to your normal learning practice. As you begin to read and interact online, you may find yourself following links down many different paths not always relevant to your focus. You may start with a tweet from a trusted source in your network that takes you to an article that links to an opposing blog post, which might lead you to a YouTube video or a new magazine article. It will test your ability to keep moving in the right direction by building your own curriculum, textbook, and classroom as you go. The ability for us to make almost all of the decisions about our own learning really is the powerful potential of these technologies—and will require focus and organization.

Networks also require *balance* in the sense that we need to turn everything off from time to time as well. One of the starkest shifts over the last ten years is the constant access to information and conversations that we now have. It's imperative that we practice balance, in whatever form that takes. For instance, we know some networked learners who turn off everything at 6:00 p.m. every evening, or who put limits on how much time they spend on Facebook or Twitter every day. Others take longer breaks, weeks even, to try to maintain some perspective between their online and offline worlds. We would also argue, however, that most educators are currently out of balance in that they don't spend enough time connected. Fifteen minutes online a day, on average, can get you started down this road pretty well, but if you find yourself spending hours online at the expense of your family and friends, it's probably a good time to reevaluate.

Regular reflection on your network interactions is a good thing. From time to time, assess the learning that's coming from your time spent online. Are the people you are connected to adding value? Are you organizing the information and knowledge that you are extracting from those interactions in helpful ways? Are you making the most of your time online, or are you finding yourself lost in the sea of information and conversations? These types of questions can help you improve the "signal to noise" ratio in your practice.

Finally, remember, too, that our *face-to-face networks* are still important in our learning. In this chapter, we emphasize the virtual connections that we can make, but we believe very strongly that the personal interactions you have with passionate learners in your real lives are equally as important. In fact, as intentional as we may be in finding and creating contacts and connections online, there is still a great deal to be said for the more serendipitous learning that can take place in staff rooms and conference halls and other face-to-face settings. The good news is that we can now use online tools to extend those face-to-face learning relationships, allowing them to grow and deepen even when we're not together in the same room.

Obviously, this is not a linear process; we don't start with one of these ideas and build in the others in a lock-step way. We won't try to boil down learning practices into their easiest common denominator, as if there is a formula or a consistent "Ten Steps to Success" program when it comes to learning. There isn't. Yes, it does mean that you are going to have to find the time in what is undoubtedly an already jam-packed schedule to turn the network learning concept into reality in your own life. But as we said before, if you can find just fifteen minutes a day, or an hour or two a week, you can reap many of the benefits that these online spaces offer—really! Most importantly, however, you'll gain the context that your students need you to have in order to help them make sense of their own online learning lives.

The Tools

So let's get started building that network, shall we? In this section, we're going to look at five specific online tools you can choose from that can help you create, navigate, and grow your own personal learning network in safe, effective, and ethical ways: Twitter, Diigo, Google Reader, Blogger, and Facebook. We've chosen these tools carefully because we think they offer the greatest potential for connections and shifted practice for most people out there. That's not to say these are the only ones to consider, as one look at Jane Hart's annual list of the "Top 100 Tools for Learning" quickly makes clear (Hart, 2010). But these five create what we think is a solid foundation for the types of interactions that will lead to effective, vibrant learning networks.

Having said that, we're aware that any discussion of specific online tools is difficult. Tools change; they go away, and newer, sometimes better ones emerge. Just in the course of writing this book, in fact, came news that one of our long-time favorite tools, the social bookmarking site Delicious, was potentially going to be shuttered unless Yahoo, its owner, could find a buyer. (Luckily for us, that news came before our final deadline.) So while we are going to offer up some starting points for your networked learning tool kit, please remember: it's the connections that matter. Networks are resilient to whatever changes the tools might throw their way and will continue to exist.

While the main goals for these tools are to share, interact, collaborate, and collect, please remember that your own use should be guided by the two undeniable realities of Internet participation. First, nothing that you post online can ever be assumed to be 100 percent private. Even though we may check the "Friends and Family" box on Facebook or a photo-sharing site like Flickr, there's nothing really stopping those to whom we give access from taking that story or picture and sharing it in their own networks. It would be great to say that we can trust everyone we interact with, but if you put something in digital form, you can't assume it won't be shared. That goes for regular old email as well.

The second rule you need to remember is that once you hit the "publish" button with any of these tools, you can't take it back. The speed at which information travels these days means that whatever you share online might be seen by thousands of people in even just a few seconds. Google caches every page on the web, and RSS readers (which we'll talk about later) are constantly fetching new content from the spaces we publish. You may hit "delete" less than a minute after you tweet, but you can never assume it's totally gone away. So make sure what you share isn't going to get you in trouble. You never know who will see it.

Now we know that those two realities are enough to make many of you put down (or turn off) this book and walk away from this whole conversation, and that's a totally reasonable and sane reaction. It's hard to get comfortable with "planet-scale sharing" as author Clay Shirky (2010) calls it, especially when it's so different from what we're used to. But remember, this isn't a race; there's no prize for being first. You can take all the time you need to ease into these tools in ways that make sense for you as long as you're moving forward, exploring, learning, and connecting. People are less concerned about your mistakes than you might think.

Here's the flip side: that "you never know who will see it" part is in some way also what makes this moment so amazing from a learning standpoint. That blog post you wrote showing how your kids designed solar panels for your community's town hall may be read by another teacher half a world away on his cell phone, causing him to think about a similar project for his own students. Who knows? He might send you an email asking if your classes can collaborate on the next project.

Finally, we're going to remind you again to resist the urge to think too much about your classrooms while reading and learning about the following tools. We'll be looking at all of that in depth in the next chapter. We're convinced that until you have built your own networks and have seen these types of learning experiences for yourself, it's really difficult to use these tools well to build connections in the classroom. Be selfish at the start; do this for yourself first, and your students will benefit greatly later.

With that, let's dive in, or at least stick a few toes in the networked learning waters.

Twitter

Twitter has been one of the fastest-growing social tools since 2008, and it's not hard to see why. In a nutshell, Twitter allows you to write and publish a "tweet" about what you're doing or thinking at the moment in 140 characters or less. It's a short snippet of your existence that is then seen by the people who have chosen to "follow" you. For most, that means a few dozen to a few hundred friends and family members who might want to keep abreast of what you're up to at any given moment. For others, however, it might mean thousands or even tens of thousands (and, yes, millions) who want to learn from you and with you.

Most people who hear about Twitter for the first or second (or third) time just can't understand what all the fuss is about. It seems silly—who would want to read something like "Oh gosh, the baby just threw up on me!" or "Little Johnny just hit a home run!"? Nice to know, but it's not compelling content that will have anyone coming back for more.

What if you thought of Twitter as a place to share not just your life but the conversations and content that really make you think about whatever your passions are? What if you used it as a way to disseminate the best content you find to those followers? Even more importantly, what if the people who you follow on Twitter did the same for you? All of a sudden, it's not hard to see how Twitter can become an interesting (and sometimes overwhelming) way of connecting and collecting around the subjects you find most important. In fact, a 2010 study showed that 55 percent of the people who use Twitter use it to share links to news, and that number is growing (Scola, 2010).

For example, in March of 2011, Alec Couros (@courosa on Twitter), a professor at the University of Regina in Saskatchewan, posted this tweet: "Excellent intro. to Twitter by the amazing @nancywhite on Vimeo http://vimeo.com/20008272" (Couros, 2011). The link takes his followers to an eight-minute overview of how to get started on the tool. Or how about this one from *Edutopia*, the online magazine of the George Lucas Education Foundation: "New! Strategies for Embedding Project-Based Learning into #STEM http://bit.ly/fAaotB #scichat #edchat" (edutopia, 2011). Twitter is a great way to offer up some link love to the best content we find online.

For that reason, most of the educators we're connected to on Twitter will tell you it's one of their primary forms of DIYPD. In fact, these days it's where most educators seem to start when building their networks. Part of it is ease of use, but a bigger part may be that the 140-character limit creates an opportunity to participate without putting too much of yourself out there. How dangerous can it be to send out links to high-quality reading that others might find interesting and learn from, even if your name is attached to it? Answer: not very. Once you get the hang of how to start connecting with other Twitterers, your networks can grow very quickly. Tens of millions of people now have active Twitter accounts, and thousands of educators of all stripes are participating there as well.

One note before we get to the "how-to" part. We sincerely want you to pursue this network-building exercise in the context of whatever your passions are, but for the sake of simplicity, we're going to use the education community as the primary example in this book. Along the way, we'll provide some suggestions for more general connecting around your personal interests.

Getting Started

Start your Twitter journey at www.twitter.com by clicking on the "Sign Up" button in the right column. The short little form on the next page is all you have to fill in to get started, thankfully, but you do have some interesting decisions to make here. Without making it too painful, we're going to dive into some of the minor details in many of these processes just to make sure you get a sense of the broader implications of some of these decisions. The first is whether or not you should use your full name when signing up. The name you put in that blank will be the name associated with your account and will show up on your Twitter home page. In other words, everyone will be able to see it. Our strong recommendation is that you use your real, full name.

Why? So you can be found by people who look for you. Part of connecting effectively in this world is the breadth of your "G-portfolio"—that online resume or collection of links that comes up when someone Googles you. In the context of network building and learning, it really helps to be findable, so we're going to urge you to be yourself on Twitter (and everywhere else, for that matter). Using your real name will also make you think twice about doing something less than smart on Twitter, and that's always a good thing.

In the second line, add a username that will come up on each of your tweets. Here, you can be as creative as you like, within reason. We use willrich45 and RobMancabelli, both pretty straightforward, but we're connected to Teach42 (Steve Dembo), nashworld (Sean Nash), funnymonkey (Bill Fitzgerald), and a whole bunch of others with even stranger Twitter handles. Just be sure to pick a username that's not too strange; Twitter will be a part of your digital footprint online, don't forget. After that, choose a password you can remember, add your real email, decide whether or not you want others to be able to find you by searching your email (we'd suggest yes), uncheck the email updates since you'll be checking your Twitter stream regularly, and then press "Create my account." You'll have to enter the code words on the next page just to prove you're a human, and then you should be all set up.

You might want to ignore the next two Twitter pages asking for your interests and your friends and just follow our steps, which are a bit more focused way to build connections. If you do want to do a search for someone when you get to the last page, go ahead, but you might want to read ahead a bit first before doing that. The final step is to click on the link in the confirmation email that Twitter sends; then you can log in to your account, at which point your account will be active.

Before sending your own tweets, it might be good to spend some time getting your tweet feet wet by following a few people and reading what they are sharing. The first thing you want to do is find some people to follow. We've provided a fairly random list of ten folks who are great sharers on Twitter,

Alan Levine, a director at the New Media Consortium:
www.twitter.com/cogdog

Kathy Cassidy, first-grade teacher in Saskatchewan:
www.twitter.com/kathycassidy

Patrick Larkin, high school principal in Massachusetts:
www.twitter.com/bhsprincipal

Shelly Blake Plock, high school history teacher in Maryland:
www.twitter.com/teachpaperless

Pam Moran, superintendent in Virginia:
www.twitter.com/pammoran

Tom Barrett, educational consultant in the U.K.:
www.twitter.com/tombarrett

Digital Media and Learning Central, collaborative blog on education:
www.twitter.com/dmlcentral

Jay Rosen, journalism professor and media critic at NYU:
www.twitter.com/jayrosen_nyu

Edutopia, website for the George Lucas Education Foundation:
www.twitter.com/edutopia

Lee Kolbert, middle school teacher in Florida:
www.twitter.com/teachakidd

most of them in education, and you're free to start with those if you like. Go to their Twitter page (address provided) and take a look at the kinds of things they are tweeting out to their followers. Odds are, you'll find two types of tweets: (1) those that include links and (2) those that are more conversation or banter. Both are valuable in their own way.

No question, the reason we follow people on Twitter is usually because they are sharing links to great resources, whether those are blog posts, newspaper articles, new tools, or other sites or content they find valuable. In this way, they act as curators and filters, two essential roles that all of us play within our networks. Obviously, there is way too much information flowing through the web to be able to find and read even a minuscule percentage of the good stuff, so we rely on others in our networks to do much of that reading for us, select the most valuable pieces, and share what they find. They depend on us to contribute in turn. Yes, we can just be followers on Twitter, just sucking up all of the great links that come our way without ever adding to the flow ourselves, but that misses the point. This new learning world is about participation, not just consumption, and it's only with that participation piece that the real connections can happen.

That's not to say, however, that we just add content value. Part of the appeal of Twitter is that we can ask for help, make jokes, and share a little bit about our personal lives. (Yes, even occasionally when the baby spits up on us.) It's not just a learning network; it's a social network too, and it's important to be a person from time to time as well. While others may take a different tack, we tend to follow folks who are linking at least 50 percent of the time, with some exceptions for personal friends. That's how we get the most value for our time spent on Twitter.

In other words, before you decide to follow anyone on Twitter, try to assess whether or not he or she (or in some cases "it") will bring that value into the interaction. Aside from looking for the ratio of links to chatter, you might consider how many people are already following that person (the higher the number, the more potential value), take a look at the website that is linked to her Twitter profile, or do a Google search to see what comes up. Remember, you want the most bang for your Twitter time, and if you take a few extra minutes up front, you'll save time later.

If at the end of all of that you think it would be worth your time to follow that person, just go to his Twitter page (for example, www.twitter.com/willrich45 or www.twitter.com/RobMancabelli), and click the "Follow" button under his picture toward the top. From that point on, all of his tweets will show up when you go to Twitter.com and log in to your home page.

Here are a few other ways you can find others to potentially follow on Twitter:

- See who the people you follow are following. On any Twitter account page, click on the "following" link just under the person's profile at the top left corner.

- Check out the Twitter lists that people have built around various topics. Visit http://mashable.com/2009/11/02/twitter-lists-guide/ for a good how-to for creating lists.

- If you're focusing on education, visit http://twitter4teachers .pbworks.com/ on Twitter4Teachers. You'll find a list of all sorts of educators using Twitter broken down by discipline, job title, and more.

However you engage, just remember the more people you follow, the more Tweets will be coming your way. Here again, people have different strategies. Some will follow anyone who follows them, which means that if you get pretty popular on Twitter, you'll have a lot to read on your Twitter home page. Here's an important reality: *few if any Twitter users actually read all the tweets from those they follow.* Most just check in from time to time to see what's coming through the flow at any given moment. Will, for instance, limits the number of people he follows to 150, and even at that he rarely reads more than 10 percent of the daily tweets they post. Don't feel guilty if you're not keeping up; no one does.

One last piece of advice about reading Twitter: many power users don't use the Twitter home page to check their tweets. Instead, they'll use a separate app or tool like TweetDeck or Twitterific with which you can manage groups of Twitter users. Both of us use TweetDeck, which lets us separate our tweets into different users or topics to help manage the flow of tweets. You can also run searches and follow topics that have labels called hashtags associated with them—more on that in a minute. You can follow as many folks as you want, but separate out those whose tweets you really don't want to miss. And remember, you can take Twitter with you on your mobile phones since, as you probably guessed, there's an app for that.

Jumping In

Once you've spent some time getting comfortable with Twitter, it's time to start participating. When you go to www.twitter.com and log in, you'll see the "What's happening?" form at the top, which is where you'll type or paste anything you want to share with your followers. You may not have too many followers at first—we'll give you some strategies to get some in a second—but remember, the best way to begin attracting connections is to provide value on a fairly consistent basis. In an educational context at least, when you look at those who have the most followers on Twitter, all of them spend a great deal of time reading, selecting, and sharing links to interesting resources.

The easiest way to start contributing on Twitter is to "retweet." As the name suggests, when you retweet someone else's post to Twitter, you're simply sharing what someone else found with your followers. So if Alec Couros (@courosa) tweets a link to a great article about open content online, just hover your mouse on the tweet itself, and click on the "Retweet" option. Both your name and Alec's will appear on the new tweet. If characters permit, you can even add your own comments to his tweet, for example, in parentheses at the end. Twitter will let you know how many characters you have left as you type.

Most likely, you will generate your tweets using content that you read and find as you surf around the web. In those cases, links are always the key. Most links are too long, however, to make the 140-character-per-tweet limit useful, so you'll want to use some type of link-shortening tool like TinyURL (www.tinyurl.com) or bit.ly (http://bit.ly). On these sites, paste your original link into the box to generate a shorter link, which you can then use in your tweet. Another reason to use TweetDeck or similar services is because they have the link-shortening capability built in. By shortening the link, you'll have room to add the title of the page you're linking to, give some description, or ask a question—whatever you think is worth noting about the link content that fits in under 140 characters. The more you read tweets, the easier it will be to get the hang of that process.

Certainly, you'll be more motivated to tweet if you have followers reading those tweets. At the start, you're going to have to do some active marketing to let people know you've entered the Twittersphere. The easiest way to accomplish that is to personalize your tweets, which is where the @ symbol comes in handy. For instance, you could tweet "@willrich45 thought you'd find this link interesting. http://bit.ly/aQorIX" if you find an interesting resource about writing literacy in the 21st century. That way, even though Will may not be following you on Twitter, he'll see it in his "Mentions" list. In fact, just use the @ symbol whenever you want to make your tweet a reply to someone else. Odds are, those people will check out your Twitter stream, and if they find that you are sharing great links, they'll most likely follow you.

If you use the @ symbol often, you'll be interacting with all sorts of people on Twitter before you know it. Then it just becomes a matter of how much time you put in—not just reading the tweets of the people you are following, but also reading the links they send your way. It won't take long before you are swimming in interesting research, articles, and blog posts, and you'll be working to "manage, analyze, and synthesize multiple streams of simultaneous information," which NCTE (2008) wants you to be adept at.

Another way to get the most out of Twitter is to use the # symbol or "hashtag" to label certain tweets and categorize them. For instance, posts on Twitter that deal with educational reform topics often carry the hashtag "#edreform" somewhere within the Tweet—usually at the end. There are hundreds of these types of tags being used in education, and you can find a pretty complete list at the Cybrary Man site (www.cybraryman.com/edhashtags .html). In addition, you can create hashtags on the fly for conferences, workshops, or subject-specific conversations. It can be a powerful tool for organizing discussions on Twitter and for finding new people to connect to. You can also use hashtags to participate in conversations on Twitter. One of the most popular is #edchat, in which people converse in 140 characters or less using that tag to keep it as organized as a Twitter conversation can be.

Diigo

In the old days, like 2006, when we came across a site online that we wanted to save for later, we'd go up to the top of our browser and either click the "Bookmarks" button in Firefox or "Favorites" button in Internet Explorer and save the link into what, for most, became an ungodly long list of places we really meant to go back to but probably never did. Why, you might ask, is that the way we *used* to do it? Because bookmarking, like so much else on the web these days, has gone social, meaning we now do it online, not just on our computers. Now we don't just save sites for ourselves; we save them for others, too, by adding them to a public list of links that can be accessed by anyone from anywhere with a connection—not just the computer we saved them on. So that means we can all be scouring the web for great resources on, say, creating digital stories with students and can easily share those links with one another online.

That's an important shift and another step in the direction of the "if I get smarter, you get smarter" web. It means that, just like with Twitter, we see the value of working for one another and sharing the best of what we find with the world—only in this case, it's a bit more organized and a bit less interactive. Still, it's an effective connection point and an important building block for your personal network (as well as your "managing, analyzing, synthesizing" literacy.)

Two social bookmarking tools reign supreme in the education world. The first is Delicious (www.delicious.com), one of the original bookmarking sites on the web, which—as we mentioned previously—may be at risk of closing. The other is Diigo (www.diigo.com), which has become a must-use tool for educators for a variety of reasons, despite its smaller user base. Both have similar functions, and both make networks and groups a main feature of their use. Because of the uncertainty with Delicious and because Diigo actually has more functionality, we're going to focus on the latter in this section.

Getting Started

As with most of these tools, Diigo is relatively easy to use, and you can get up and running in literally about five minutes. For the more nuanced uses of Diigo, you can always do a search on YouTube to find some "how-to" videos. To start, just go to www.diigo.com and click on the blue "Get Started Now" button in the middle of the homepage. (Just to the right of the button is a small text link that says "Educator? Get started here." After you've logged in, you'll want to use that link to apply for a free educator upgrade. Visit http://help.diigo.com/teacher-account/faq to get the scoop on those accounts.) First, fill in the form to create your account, and then check your email for a link to activate the account. Once activated, you'll only be a couple of steps from starting to save all those great sites you find on the web.

The first thing you want to do is add the Diigo toolbar to your browser. Just click on the "Tools" link at the top right of the page, and you should land on a page that gives you a link to install it in whatever browser you are using. (Safari users will need to use the "Diigolet" button instead; just follow the links to install it.) It is a pretty painless procedure, and when you're done, you should see either the toolbar or a Diigo button in your browser.

Jumping In

Once you have your account set up and your toolbar buttons installed, it's time to start bookmarking. If you're following great sharers on Twitter, you will already be getting lots of links worth saving to your Diigo account. The process to do so couldn't be easier. First, make sure the page you want to save is open in your current browser window or tab. Then, even though this next step is optional, take a look at the page and try to determine the best paragraph or two of text that neatly sum up the article. Highlight that text by clicking and dragging your cursor over it while clicking on your mouse or touchpad.

Next, while your text is still highlighted, click on the "Bookmark" button that appears on the Diigo toolbar. This may vary depending on the browser you use. If you don't see the "Bookmark" option, click on the Diigo icon that you do see, and you'll most likely find it there. A Diigo form should pop up that shows the address of the site, the title, and the section of text you highlighted. You can choose to keep your bookmark private, though that kind of defeats the purpose: Diigo will be one way people can connect with you if your bookmarks are public. You can also save a version of the entire page in your Diigo account by checking "Cache," just in case the page gets taken down at some point in the future.

Next comes the "Tags" section, and from a "managing streams of information" standpoint, it may be the most important field on the form. Unlike old taxonomies that others created to help us organize information, we now have to take on that job ourselves. It's not as neat or as linear, and what works for you may not work for someone else, but the moment calls for each of us to begin to "tag" or add keywords to the content we find, create, and share so that we—and others with similar interests—can find it more easily later.

You can add as many tags as you like, but most people add between three and seven, depending on the resource. They can be general, as in "education," "learning," or "21st_Century_Skills," or they can be unique to your own needs. For instance, if you want to collect bookmarks collaboratively with your class, you might all use a tag like "jfkhsaphistory1" (Can you figure out what that means?), or if you're running a conference, you could use "educon2011." Whatever tags you use, enter them without commas, separated only by spaces. Diigo will create a list of all of your tags that you can access on your Diigo page (which, by the way, is www.diigo.com/user /your_user_name). Even better, you'll be able to search your bookmarks by the tags or by multiple tags as well.

Here is the cool thing about Diigo: you can also add highlights and sticky notes on any of the pages you bookmark, and if you make those notes and highlights public, any other Diigo users who land on the page can see and interact with them. (You'll notice highlights and notes when you start browsing around after installing Diigo as well. Visit **go.solution-tree.com/technology** for examples.) We know many teachers who have begun to deconstruct individual web pages using the notes and highlights functions with their students (but only after they themselves have played with Diigo for a while, of course).

Really, that's about it when it comes to saving bookmarks, but that's not the end of our Diigo conversation. Diigo can also be a place where you begin connecting with others who share your interests and are sharing their bookmarks. It's not nearly as conversational or social as Twitter, to be sure, but it is a place where you can begin to mine a great deal of resources if you are "networked" with great Diigoers. There are a couple of ways to do this, but let's start with the most straightforward. When you're logged in to the Diigo site, just click on the "My Network" link, and you'll be guided through a process where you can find other users with similar interests. Much like Twitter, as you add people to your network, you'll be able to easily follow all of the links they add to their Diigo accounts. If you build your network well, it's almost like having a whole research team working for you constantly. Obviously, you'll want to be a part of that team as well.

As always, there are a number of great resources to learn about Diigo online. Aside from those at www.diigo.com and the many quality tutorials on YouTube, you might want to check out the "Diigo" tag at Delicious (www .delicious.com/tag/diigo), where you'll find the latest great bookmarks about the service. And don't forget to explore Diigo's many already-created groups where educators are sharing their best links with one another (http://groups .diigo.com/index). It's another great way of making connections with other passionate educators.

Google Reader

One of the most powerful tools for gathering information is one you may not have heard of. It's called RSS, or "Real Simple Syndication," and if you take a little time to make it a part of your daily practice, it will change the way you think about information and learning.

The concept is pretty straightforward: RSS allows you to subscribe for free to "feeds" of information so that, just like the newspaper that ends up in your driveway each morning, the latest blog posts, bookmarks, and even tweets automatically get collected in your RSS "reader." For instance, if you want the most recent writings about school reform as posted by Diane Ravitch and Deborah Meier in their great blog *Bridging Differences*, you can subscribe to that blog, and whenever they update, the posts automatically come right to your reader. That means that you can collect a great deal of the best, most relevant content being produced on the web into one space for easy managing, analyzing, and synthesizing whenever you're ready to do so.

As much as RSS creates an opportunity for us to expand our connections, however, it also poses a huge challenge: it's almost too easy to start building your own "Daily Me," as some have called it, and it's not hard to feel quickly overloaded by information. So a bit of a caveat and a reminder that you have heard from us before: start slowly, and know that you don't have to read everything that comes your way via RSS. The more focused you can make the experience, the better—not only for your own learning, but also for your ability to teach and model RSS to your students and colleagues.

Getting Started

Once again, the basics here are pretty straightforward. While there are a number of RSS readers, we're going to suggest you use Google Reader, a free tool that comes with your Google account. If you don't have a Google account, just go to www.google.com, click on "Sign In" at the top right of the screen. On the next page, click on "Create an Account Now" just below the sign-in form. The process is very easy, and once you've completed it, not only do you have a reader but you also have a Gmail account, which is an email account through Google; free blogs at Blogger; free documents, calendars, spreadsheets, and presentations at Google Docs; and a whole bunch more.

Your personalized, totally private Google Reader will be at www.google .com/reader and will show up whenever you are logged in. You might want to put a link to it on your browser toolbar for easy access when you want to read what posts and articles have arrived. You might also want to create a popup on your Google calendar for the first few weeks to remind you to visit. RSS is the type of tool that works best for you when it becomes a regular part of your network practice.

The only real "how-to" part of RSS is finding and adding subscriptions to follow. To use the *Bridging Differences* example from earlier, if after reading through some of the recent posts you decide that you want to subscribe, just copy the address of the blog (http://blogs.edweek.org/edweek/Bridging

-Differences/), open Google Reader, click on the "Add a Subscription" button, paste the address into the form that pops up, and click "Add." The name of the blog will be added to your subscriptions list in the lower part of the left-hand column. That's it. Now every time a new blog post is added to the *Bridging Differences* site, a copy of it will automatically be sent to your reader. You'll know when new posts arrive because the blog name will turn bold and you'll see a number in parentheses showing how many new posts have arrived.

When you click on the subscription, the posts themselves will show up in the right-hand pane. You'll see a set of options at the bottom of each post that will allow you to email the link to someone, star it as a favorite, and even add tags if you want to organize the links. From a networked learner scenario, however, you might want to think about clicking on the links that you find most interesting to open them in your browser, saving them to Diigo, and maybe even sharing them on Twitter. Being a great filter of information for your network is an important role.

Jumping In

So what else can you subscribe to with Google Reader, aside from blogs? Well, a lot of stuff, actually. Let's say you are interested in the rain forest and you want to keep track of any global news relating to that topic. You can go to Google News (www.google.com/news), do a search for "rain forest," take the address of the page where the search results come up, copy it, and add it to Google Reader. Then you'll get a link to every article published about rain forests from around the world as they occur. If you want to narrow your search in Google News, and you probably will, just click on the "Advanced Search" link to limit your query to a particular country, a specific newspaper, and more.

By using Google Blog Search (http://blogsearch.google.com), you can search all the blogs in the world. Once again, if you take the address of the search result and add it to your reader, you'll have a constant flow of blog posts about the rain forest coming your way. If you find some blogs that write about the rain forest on a regular basis, you might subscribe to those as well.

You can also track all of the great sites about rain forests that people are saving to Diigo in your RSS reader. Just take the Diigo address for the tag "rainforest" (www.diigo.com/tag/rainforest), and add it to your reader. If you want to collect all the tweets with the hashtag #rainforest, you can go to http://search.twitter.com, enter the tag, copy the address of the results, and add it to Google Reader. Want pictures and movies? You can subscribe to Flickr photos and YouTube videos about the rain forest as well. Just do the searches, and, well, you should have the idea by now.

Finally, don't forget that one of the keys to building your learning network is interacting with the content you find or, in this case, content that finds you. Don't hesitate to click on those really interesting blog posts that come into your reader, and perhaps leave some comments for those bloggers. The more you enter those conversations and start sharing your own ideas, the more connections you'll make.

Blogger

The weblog, or "blog," is the granddaddy of social media, if there is such a thing. Way back at the turn of the 21st century, blogs starting popping up as a way for individuals to publish their thoughts online at the click of a button (no HTML or FTP stuff required). It was like sending an email to the world. More importantly, blogs became a place where readers could actually respond to those ideas. Currently, you'll find over 200 million blogs online in various stages of use, and on many of them, you'll find some of the best writing and thinking anywhere. Blogs are a powerful writing and multimedia tool that more and more educators are beginning to bring into their classrooms. In general, blogs are a tremendous tool for synthesizing ideas, connecting to other teachers and resources, and with a little time and patience, developing a conversation around the topics you care about the most. But even more importantly, they are a great way for each of us to reflect on our own practice and experiences in our schools and classrooms.

In fact, the use of blogs in classrooms actually has some research support behind it. A 2010 University of New Hampshire study found that "regularly creating blog entries had a positive impact on learners' writing fluency and increased their motivation to write for a broad audience" (Lee, 2010). The abstract of another study from Northwestern State University in Louisiana found that a blog "enhances curriculum, supports cognitive abilities, and creates a positive learning community" (McBride & King, 2010). In addition, the study found that "writing skills of elementary age students can improve because the tool excites the student and is already a familiar mode of communication" (McBride & King, 2010).

Don't kid yourself; blogging can be hard work. It takes time to read and think and synthesize and write. But for many, the process is worth it, not just because it's good learning work that can produce some "intellectual sweat" from time to time, but also because it definitely gets you to grapple more deeply with the whole shift around transparent participation that's occurring. Blogging is also one of the best ways to fully understand these shifts in the sense of creating great pedagogy and curriculum around the use of blogs in the classroom. If we're going to use the NCTE definition again, blogs are where we "analyze and synthesize" as well as connect.

Here is a bit of history. Blogs arrived around 2000 and created the foundation for the Web 2.0 phenomenon, the explosion of online tools that allowed people to easily connect online. In the early days of blogs, they were seen as mostly online journals or diaries, and for some, that's still how they are used. For most, however, blogs are now places of exposition where the essay has taken on a new life, complete with links and multimedia. On our blogs, we opine, we curate, we filter, we connect, and we do it in a way that is open to the world to see and interact with.

That last part is daunting, and it's what stops many from starting their own blogs. An oft-heard refrain by newcomers is "But what do I have to say that people would be interested in?" It's a valid question, but the truth is that if you are writing about your passion, you'll have readers. It may take a while, but in the world of Twitter and instant connections, it won't take as long as you think. In the past year, we've seen many Tony Baldasaros come out of nowhere to become important parts of the conversation; it all comes down to a willingness to learn, test ideas, and share stories with what most will tell you is a very welcoming community—no matter the topic.

Besides, no one is saying that you have to wax philosophic on your blog five times a week. Many folks just use their blogs to post short commentaries on links that they've found, while others use it as a portfolio space for photos they've taken or videos they've created. Some post fairly regularly, others just a few times a month. Do whatever works for you, as long as there is some level of engagement and participation that helps you grow the connections in your network and helps you understand the potentials for your students.

Getting Started

Before you create your own blog, however, we're going to suggest you take some time to read other blogs first. Remember, you can use Google Blog Search (http://blogsearch.google.com) to find folks who are blogging about your interests. When you do, don't just look at the ways the bloggers weave in references to the things they have read or found on the web. Pay attention to the writing style (most are pretty informal) and the ways the bloggers use pictures and multimedia. Look at the overall design and feel of the space, how often they post, the types of comments they get, and links to other places where you might connect with them. In other words, do some analysis. Then, when you feel compelled to do so, we would encourage you to leave some comments and get into some conversations. Again, when you comment, use your real name.

When you're ready, the easiest way to start a personal blog is to use Google's Blogger (www.blogger.com), especially if you've gone through the process of setting up a Google account already. Just go to Blogger, sign in with your Google information, and it will take you through an easy setup process that will have you blogging in under five minutes. As always, there are a large number of getting-started videos about Blogger on YouTube, but remember to think carefully about the name of your blog, and don't be shy about using your real name when you set it up. You want to be findable. Blogger also has a whole bunch of creative themes to choose from, so feel free to experiment a bit.

Jumping In

More important than the setup, however, is the process of blogging. Where do you get ideas to write about? How do you begin to make connections? How do you "market" your blog posts? Ideas spring from the things you read; you get things to read from Twitter, Diigo, and Google Reader; and you share your blog posts using those tools as well. In this way, in fact, Twitter is one of the most powerful tools to disseminate your blog posts and attract readers. In other words, once you get the hang of it, these tools can all work in concert to begin building a really powerful learning network.

While it's probably obvious already, the key technical ingredient to creating connections while blogging is the link, and many of your blog posts should be filled with them. If you're writing about something that you read, be it a newspaper article, a bookmark, or a post on someone else's blog, make sure to create a link to that piece within your post. If you do that, two things (if not more) happen. First, you add valuable context to whatever it is that you are writing about. If your readers want to read more about the topic or simply check your logic, they can, with one simple click. The other reason is that, through the wonders of the web, the bloggers you link to will automatically find out that you are writing about them, and that means more potential for network building. This type of notification is called a "trackback," if you want to learn more about how that works.

There's nothing wrong with posts that are primarily reflection or narrative, sharing experiences that you feel are important in your own learning and that might be of interest to your readers. Even if you don't have many readers at the outset, have faith that they will come if you are consistent in writing on your blog and in using these other tools to grow your connections and, as a by-product, share your blogging to a wider audience. Make sure to interact with your readers as they begin to comment on your posts; responding in the comment thread is a great way to deepen the conversation and connection.

Facebook

No question, Facebook is the eight-hundred-pound gorilla of *social* networking these days, having left MySpace in the dust, at least in terms of North American participation. Despite numerous missteps surrounding privacy and personal information sharing, Facebook has become proof positive that social networks are here to stay, with over five hundred million active users at this writing and adding over five hundred thousand new users a day. It's mind-boggling to think about.

Keeping in mind that our focus at this stage is on building our own learning networks rather than finding ways to use these tools in the classroom, Facebook is an important site for all educators to experience, if for no other reason than to help their students understand the potentials and the pitfalls. It's also a great way to start connecting online, because on Facebook you network with people you already know. While different people have begun to use Facebook for different purposes (such as marketing, activism, and politics), at its core it's still about "friending" the people in your life you want to connect with. In that respect, at least, it's not about sharing to the world at large. Just remember, however, that our two golden rules of online interaction apply here as well.

Getting Started

Getting set up on Facebook isn't rocket science, so we won't spend a lot of time on that process here. Just go to www.facebook.com and fill out the form. You'll have the chance to connect with folks already in your email contact list if you'd like. This does require you to share your email password with Facebook, however—something many are not willing to do. Once you've gone through the login process, you'll be able to search for people already on Facebook, create groups of family members or colleagues, and update your friends on what's going on in your life.

Jumping In

The key to Facebook, as with any of these tools, is using it appropriately and using it well. For all sorts of reasons, it's best not to friend current students, even though you may actually be friends with them in real life. And it's best to not use your Facebook page as a place to vent your frustrations with the system or your colleagues. Remember, even though you can configure your Facebook privacy settings so that only your "friends" can see your page, you have to think of it as a public space. Similarly, feel free to post pictures to your page (over a million go up every day), but you might not want to add any of you at a keg party wearing a pirate costume for obvious reasons. Facebook is also a great place to connect with some of the professional organizations that might be associated with your interests. In education, you might try the *Edutopia* page (www.facebook.com/edutopia), the ISTE page (www.facebook.com/pages/ISTE/8828374188), or even the National Council of Teachers of English (www.facebook.com/ncte.org) page, among many others. These are great spaces to meet and learn with others in your discipline or subject area.

Obviously, the privacy concerns that so many folks have about Facebook are real and shouldn't be ignored; you can buy a number of well-written books on the subject, in fact. While we'd love to go into some depth over those concerns, we don't have the time or space to do the conversation justice, especially since things have a tendency to shift very quickly in this type of discussion. A free download titled *The (Very) Unofficial Facebook Privacy Guide* will serve as a great primer for your foray into the choices you can make concerning privacy on your site (Alcorn, n. d.).

Finally, one last bit of caution regarding Facebook: remember that ultimately anything you post to Facebook is owned by Facebook and can be removed at any time by its staff. For this and a number of other reasons, some important voices such as Tim Berners-Lee, the web's inventor, and others have been speaking out against a growing trend to use the site as a one-stop shop for content creation and publishing. Sure, Facebook makes this whole networking thing easier, but from a learning standpoint, that doesn't necessarily mean better. Learning on the web is about participating in many spaces in different ways, and there is a real danger, we think, in tying too much of our work to one particular site.

Levels of Participation

Once you have established your networks, how will you use them? We feel strongly that every educator would be well served to be a participant in these spaces to some degree. If we've succeeded in building a compelling case around the shift to networked, passion-based learning online, then how can educators choose not to participate? Remember, our students are already taking part in social networks like Facebook in droves, but there is a big distinction between the social interactions at Facebook and the learning interactions we're talking about here. The reality right now is that most of our students have no one teaching them or modeling for them what sustained, passion-based, self-directed learning in networked online spaces can be. They are not the "digital natives" some would have you believe when it comes to the networked *learning* aspect of all of this. They're immigrants just like we are.

Let's also be clear about something else: just as generic learning is on its way out in the classroom, the ways in which we explore these environments for ourselves will be as unique as our own personalities and proclivities. While we'll provide an easy, step-by-step process to follow, no two of us will follow the exact same path to success. In essence, you'll be travelling down your own unique learning road here, which is as it should be.

If you want to get some sense of how people in general participate in online networks, the "ladder" (fig. 2.1) gives a pretty good overview of the different levels of activity.

In other words, there are lots of ways to get involved. We would also suggest that the farther up you can move on this ladder, the better. That's not to say you can't find value in participating at the lower rungs, especially at first. But those "take, not give" activities won't do much for growing a learning network. In our experience, becoming a creator affords the most opportunity to experience rich connections, so think about the starting points outlined here and the ways you might work your way up. And remember, it's not a race; no one is grading you, and everyone will travel a different path.

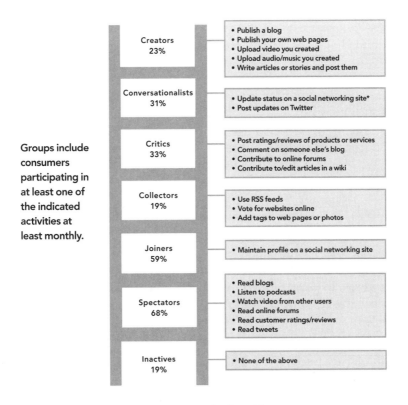

Groups include consumers participating in at least one of the indicated activities at least monthly.

| Creators 23% | • Publish a blog
• Publish your own web pages
• Upload video you created
• Upload audio/music you created
• Write articles or stories and post them |

| Conversationalists 31% | • Update status on a social networking site*
• Post updates on Twitter |

| Critics 33% | • Post ratings/reviews of products or services
• Comment on someone else's blog
• Contribute to online forums
• Contribute to/edit articles in a wiki |

| Collectors 19% | • Use RSS feeds
• Vote for websites online
• Add tags to web pages or photos |

| Joiners 59% | • Maintain profile on a social networking site |

| Spectators 68% | • Read blogs
• Listen to podcasts
• Watch video from other users
• Read online forums
• Read customer ratings/reviews
• Read tweets |

| Inactives 19% | • None of the above |

Base: U.S. online adults

*Conversationalists participate in at least one of the indicated activities at least weekly.

Source: Used with permission from Forrester Research. Adapted from Anderson and Bernoff (2010) and Elliott (2010).

Figure 2.1: A ladder of activity for users of online social media.

Making It Work

So what does this all look like in your own personal learning practice? Since no two people are going to have the exact same networks or the exact same interactions, there's no one right answer to that question. You can assume, however, that the way you learn in your network is going to look and feel different from your current learning practice. You're creating your own learning path here, and little about this has a decidedly linear, step-by-step feel. If you begin to use these tools fairly regularly, you'll see that your Twitter network will seep into your blog network and Facebook connections as well as those you have on Diigo and elsewhere. Pretty soon the whole thing will begin to become a part of your learning workflow—one network of integrated parts that work seamlessly together. We know that might seem like a long way off for those of you who are just starting down this road, but as we said, these days there are a lot of Tony Baldasaros out there—people who are participating in pretty extensive networks after just a few short weeks and months.

Effective participation has a consistent look and feel, however personalized or general that may be. For instance, simply reading all of the links and resources provided by your network is a good first start, but as figure 2.1 (page 55) implies, responding and creating are how you will reap real benefits. If there is one mantra we would suggest you keep in mind when using these tools, it's simply this: add value. As you read, reflect, and learn from the flow, also remember to ask, "Would this be useful for others who are connected to me in my network?" If the answer is yes, then you might think about tweeting it out, saving it as a bookmark, or even writing a blog post about it. While most of the value you add will be focused around your professional interests, don't forget that occasionally, a more personal level of sharing is integral to effective participation as well. It might be a picture you put up on Twitter (using www.twitpic.com, for instance) that shows the great-looking bread you baked for Thanksgiving or the kids dressed up in their Halloween costumes. Or it might be a blog post describing a conversation about education that you overheard at the local diner. In other words, we want to see your humanity as it adds to our sense of who you are and what lens you bring to the larger conversation. So mix it up from time to time; your connections will deepen.

Almost all of these tools work on mobile devices. While we haven't really discussed the growing presence of smartphones and iPad-like devices, all of them have apps or software that make tweeting, blogging, and Facebooking pretty much a breeze. So next time you're standing in line at the checkout, and you have a few spare seconds, see what your network is up to and perhaps "favorite" a few of those tweets or items in your Google Reader for later in the day or week.

Finally, understand that along with the challenges to staying focused that we touched on in chapter 1, there are other acute shifts we need to reflect on regularly. For instance, this personal transformation is emotional as well as intellectual. Learning how to use the tools is only part of the process, and for some, it may be the easy part. The real test of your commitment will come as you ride the emotional roller coaster of participation that every learning network beginner experiences.

At first, there will be days when you wonder, "Why am I doing this?" In fact, you may feel like you're tweeting and blogging to an empty room. You may write a long blog post that articulates an important part of your worldview and really struggle with the fear that comes with clicking on the "publish" button. Your first few blog posts may not get any comments, and your first two hundred tweets may just float into the ether. But these first steps are a great opportunity to see what works for you and what doesn't, and to get a feel for your own reactions to putting more of yourself online. Allow yourself time to get acclimated, to start understanding how these interactions change things. Enjoy that initial quiet, and trust that if you participate regularly and "add value," others will find you and your anonymity will soon fade. A connection with someone in another part of the world will exhilarate you, and an educational idea will take you to a whole new level of thinking about your field. People you have never met will thank you for contributing to their learning, and you'll participate in regular conversations with the same familiar rhythms of your daily face-to-face interactions. Your network will grow, and your learning will never be the same.

CHAPTER 3

IMPLEMENTING A NETWORKED CLASSROOM

Seventh-/eighth-grade teacher Clarence Fisher has an interesting way of describing his classroom in Snow Lake, Manitoba. As he tells it, it has "thin walls," meaning that despite being eight hours north of the nearest metropolitan airport, his students are getting out into the world on a regular basis, using the web to connect and collaborate with students in places around the globe. The name of Clarence's blog, *Remote Access*, sums up nicely the opportunities that his students have in their networked classroom.

"Learning is only as powerful as the network it occurs in," Clarence says. "No doubt, there is still value in the learning that occurs between teachers and students in classrooms. But the power of that learning is more solid and more relevant at the end of the day if the networks and the connections are larger" (C. Fisher, personal communication, November 23, 2010).

Without question, Clarence exemplifies that notion of the "networked learner" that we talked about in the last chapter. Aside from reflecting on his life and his practice on his blog, he uses Twitter to grow his network, uses Delicious to capture and share bookmarks, and makes other tools like Skype and YouTube a regular part of his learning life. In other words, he's deeply rooted in the learning networks he advocates for his students.

"It's changed everything for me as a learner," he says. "I teach in a small school of 145 kids, so I don't know what it's like to have a lot of colleagues. I can't imagine closing my door and having to generate all of these ideas on my own."

Clarence helps his students create these networked interactions at every turn. A few years ago, his students collaborated with a classroom in Los Angeles to study S. E. Hinton's novel *The Outsiders*, using Skype for live conversations and blogs to capture their reflections on both the story and the interactions. More recently, his students studied *The Book Thief* by Markus Zusak with a class of Ontario students, listening online as their teachers read parts of the book aloud while conducting a chat in the background filled with questions, reflections, and predictions as to what would happen next. Over the years, his students have worked with kids in Australia, Brazil, Argentina, and China, just to name a few.

But here's the thing: while Clarence may initially be the one to make these connections, most of the networking quickly starts coming from his students. As he was beginning to explore the idea of the "thin-walled" classroom back in 2006, he wrote the following on his blog:

> The connections have had very little to do with me. I've provided access, direction, and time, but little else. I have not had to make elaborate plans with teachers, nor have I had to coordinate efforts, parceling out contacts and juggling numbers. It is all about the kids. The kids have made contacts. They have begun to find voices that are meaningful to them, and voices they are interested in hearing more from. They are becoming connectors and mavens, drawing together strings of a community. They are beginning to expect to work in this way. They want to know what the people in their network are saying, to hear about their lives and their learning. They want feedback on their own learning, and they want to know they are surrounded by a community who hears them. They make no distinction about class, about race, about proficiency in English, or about geography. They are only interested in the conversation and what it means to them. (Fisher, 2006)

That's a very different picture from what happens in most traditional classrooms, but it captures the essence of what student (and teacher) learning can look like in schools these days. Thin walls expand the classroom, and in the process deepen our understanding and practice of all of those 21st century skills that we referenced earlier—the critical thinking, the problem solving, and the rest. As students begin to experience the powerful pull of connections to other students and teachers outside of their physical spaces, they also begin to see the world writ large as a part of their daily learning lives. Just as Clarence says these networks "changed everything for me as a learner," they also change our interactions with the kids we teach, the way we think about classrooms, and the way we see the world. Those are big statements, we know, but we see these shifts being played out every day in profound ways. More and more, they reflect the real world of learning that our students will graduate into, whether we help them get there or not.

What Changes

As always, the change starts with us. If we truly commit to the idea of creating a networked classroom, we also need to commit to changing the way we think about our roles in those classrooms. To put it plainly, as George Siemens suggests, "social and technological networks subvert the classroom-based role of the teacher" (2010). When students can find content from many different sources, and when we can literally bring scientists and researchers into the classroom to interact directly with students, the traditional "teacher as expert" model is turned on its head (Siemens, 2010). We're talking about a shift in roles. Instead of being the smartest people in the room, we need to be effective connectors for our students, able to sift through all those potential teachers online, find the most relevant ones, and effectively use technologies such as blogs, Skype, or others to bring them to our students. As Siemens says, we also need to be transparent about the process by modeling safe and effective techniques for connecting and learning with others. That all comes with being networked learners ourselves.

In turn, all of this changes the classroom culture itself. Instead of the teacher "teaching" and the students "learning," teachers and students become co-learners as well as co-teachers in the process. The classroom begins to become a community of learners in which each person takes some responsibility for achieving curricular goals and outcomes. In some cases, students become classroom "scribes," as Vancouver math teacher Darren Kuropatwa called it, rotating responsibilities for taking notes on the daily lessons and adding links, graphics, discussion questions, and other content to the class blog after class ends. As Darren explains it, "Over the course of the semester, the scribe posts will grow into the textbook for the course; written by students for students" (Kuropatwa, 2006). In a similar scenario, students work collaboratively to capture notes and other resources on a wiki page or in a shared Google Doc, taking what might otherwise be a linear, text-heavy book and turning it into a compilation of videos, virtual tours, interviews, blog posts, journal articles, and a whole host of other connected resources for further study related to the topic at hand. In the process, students find other potential teachers that may be suitable to bring into the classroom for live discussions or collaboration.

In other words, we need to unlearn much of what teachers historically have done, and instead begin to craft new roles and expectations for ourselves in the classroom. As Siemens suggests, we are now one of many teachers in our students' networked lives, though no doubt a prominent one among other people or resources. In that respect, our role becomes one of helping students organize their own learning and navigate the complexities of finding and connecting their own nodes of learning in ways that serve them well. We also must act as expert filters, demonstrating the fundamental literacies around information as we find, sort, synthesize, save, and share the most relevant resources in our own learning. And we must be transparent models of learning in these networked spaces. Our students need to be able to access our contributions, interact with them, and learn from them online.

We know the shift to the idea of "classroom as node" is not an easy one. As much as we hope we've made the case for teaching our students to be self-directed learners who can take charge of their own education, we also know they must still pass the test and achieve in traditional ways. The good news is that passing the test and becoming literate, modern learners are not mutually exclusive. We can help students achieve both goals. For those teachers who have no personal context for networked learning, getting started requires a leap of faith, but we're confident that once you've taken the time to create your own learning connections and networks, you will see a path to achieving important outcomes for your current students.

The Benefits of the Networked Classroom

Before we look at some case studies of teachers who have turned their classrooms into networked learning spaces, we want to give you some idea of what those classrooms look like. When you do eventually find yourself teaching and learning in a networked classroom, you'll also find that classroom looks and feels very different from the one that came before. In fact, there are a few qualities of new learning environments that particularly stand out. Networked classrooms are:

- Transparent

- Collaborative

- Learning centered

- Accessible

- Communication based

- Supportive of problem- or inquiry-based learning

- Driven by authentic assessment

First, networked classrooms are *transparent*. Just as individual learners need to share openly in order to foster connections, classrooms also need to open up to the world online. Why? For one, classrooms that share provide great opportunities for students to learn about participation, publishing, safety, and network building in real ways (as opposed to the fairly contrived opportunities in traditional classrooms). Instead of the project that gets displayed on the hallway bulletin board, student work can be published to a larger audience that, depending on the age and circumstance of the students, might be encouraged to interact with the work by commenting on it or perhaps even participating in the creation of improvements. Additionally, transparent classrooms are more apt to create connections with other classrooms around the world, increasing opportunities for collaboration and cultural awareness. In the same way that we need to be findable to others in order to learn with them, sharing our work and the work of our students can lead to many dots on our classroom maps.

Second, networked classrooms by their very nature are *collaborative*. At a time when we have so many potential others with whom we can learn and create, the adage "do your own work" doesn't make much sense any longer. If we remember that "none of us is as smart as all of us," we can begin to tap into the expertise of both those around us and those outside the school. Students can become teachers, helping both the adults and the kids in the room learn. Students and teachers together can begin to create meaningful things together, artifacts that have relevance and use far beyond the end of the school year. In this way, too, the primary activity within the classroom shifts from the acquisition of knowledge as individuals to the creation of knowledge with one another—knowledge that is then shared with the world.

Third, these classrooms are also *learning centered*, which means the emphasis is more on developing the skills to become lifelong, self-directed learners than on content that students are expected to stow away in their heads for recall at some future date. Again, the current educational regime still expects a good deal of that content knowledge, and at this point, we still have to make sure that our students "know" certain things. But in the spirit of helping students "create their own education," we must also focus on those learning literacies that will make them successful in a world in which there is simply far too much knowledge for any one person to know and remember.

Fourth, networked classrooms are more *accessible* in terms of the content and the students who are a part of it. Coursework is routinely posted to an online portal, be that a blog or a content management site like Moodle (http://moodle.org). Lectures might be recorded and shared online, and the class may have a designated space for students to backchannel—have text conversations—either inside or outside of class. While no one expects teachers to be on call constantly, the networked classroom reflects the idea that learning can happen anytime, anywhere. *Accessible* in this light doesn't just mean the content is available to the students and teachers in the room; it also means the content is findable to other classrooms, students, parents, and teachers who may seek to interact or collaborate in some way.

Fifth, the networked classroom is *communication based*, meaning that our students are constantly practicing oral and written communication in every interaction. Learning in networked spaces requires participating, not simply consuming passively, so students are continually engaged in a process of reading, writing, and interacting with other students and teachers and testing ideas. In this networked space, communication is not just a product of written text. As the NCTE literacies suggest, our students need to be fluent in the creation and analysis of multimedia and need to be able to use pictures, audio, and video to shape and convey ideas and knowledge.

Sixth, *problem-* or *inquiry-based learning* is more possible in networked classrooms. Many of the hallmarks of problem-based learning, such as promoting ownership and addressing large challenges, are a natural fit for the connected classroom. Students can work on real-world problems with the people trying to solve them, learning from them about the challenges in their fields and thinking about how they can contribute. This increases student engagement while sharpening the skills students will need when they finish their schooling.

Finally, these classrooms are driven by *authentic assessment*, meaning students are not just judged on quiz or test scores or traditional writing assignments. Students are doing real work for real purposes for real audiences, and the products they create are measured accordingly through self-reflection on the creation process, performances, portfolios, and a host of other ways. That's not to suggest that all forms of formative or summative assessments are abandoned, but if the emphasis of the classroom is turning toward learning and the skills to best make that happen, the expectations are difficult to measure with a bubble test or a short-answer essay.

What the Networked Classroom Looks Like

Let's take a look at some extended stories of teachers like Clarence whose teaching lives have been transformed by making the connections now possible on the web an integral part of student learning. We've tried to offer diverse stories of fairly typical teachers who are representative of the many traditional classroom instructors beginning to shift their practices in truly transformative ways. None of us come to these changes in the same way, which is as it should be, but as you'll see, there are some overarching themes that all of us share when we take on this journey.

A word of context, however: these vignettes are what Chip and Dan Heath call "destination postcards": "a vivid picture from the near-term future that shows what could be possible" (Heath & Heath, 2010, Kindle location 1103). At some point, all of these teachers were where most of you are now, without a lot of connections or even a clear picture of what learning networks are. Their evolution to these spaces was years in the making. So please resist the voice that says, "I could never be like that." You can. You will.

Anne Smith

While there are literally thousands of teachers using the web to network their classrooms in meaningful ways, few have done it better than Anne Smith, a high school English teacher at Arapahoe High School in Littleton, Colorado. A thirteen-year veteran of the classroom, Anne has experienced a huge shift over the past few years in the ways she thinks about her own learning, and that shift plays out almost every day in her role as a teacher.

"Because of the abundance of information and resources and people online, our job more than anything is to connect kids beyond the classroom," Anne says. "And a big part of that is creation of their own learning networks, through reading widely on blogs, finding literature, finding experts, connecting pieces all over the place so that their minds just don't stop thinking. It's a whole different classroom and an important way to make sure our students will be successful in life" (A. Smith, personal communication, November 3, 2010).

What's different about Anne is that she's not afraid to ask some big-name authors and experts to connect with her kids, and she's got a think-outside-the-box approach to getting the most out of those interactions.

Case in point is best-selling author Dan Pink, who has been an integral part of her students' study of his book *A Whole New Mind* since 2008. While the idea of inviting an author to blog with a class or sit for an interview on Skype is nothing new, Anne saw an opportunity to deepen the experience for her students using other educators and experts around the world to help students reflect and discuss the themes of the book. While what follows may sound complex, few of you would need more than a few hours to learn the tools to make it work for yourselves.

Here's how it worked: Pink was invited to videoconference with the school using Skype, a free, online telephone/video tool, and was interviewed by a panel of students who led a two-hour discussion about one of the chapters of the book. At the same time, Anne streamed the video Skype conversation to the world using Ustream (www.ustream.tv) so that others in her network who had seen her tweets about the event could join in virtually. In addition, while the Pink interview was taking place, her other students were using their laptops to "live blog" the event using a service called Cover it Live (www.coveritlive.com), a sort of text chatting tool that has a moderator function built in. Other folks who were watching the stream live could join in the discussion as well. (Visit **go.solution-tree.com /technology** for a great video that discusses the event's planning process and for more resources.)

These interactions didn't just occur on the day of Pink's videoconference, however. Over the course of a couple of weeks, Anne's students had "fishbowl" conversations about the other chapters; some sat in the middle of the room discussing the chapters face to face, and others in an outer circle observed and live-blogged, asking questions, reflecting, and sharing their insights online. Those classroom conversations were streamed out as well so students had a global audience for their discussions. Finally, Anne solicited the help of educators in her network to join each live blog session as a surrogate mentor, gently probing and pushing back as the text chat ensued, helping students think more deeply about the discussion.

"I want my kids to constantly go beyond the piece of paper," Anne says. "I want to teach them to constantly search for more, seek out more voices, and take advantage of the chances we have for doing that now."

On other occasions, the connections are more serendipitous, stemming from her personal network ties. Last fall, Anne read an essay titled "Schools Would Be Great if It Weren't for the Kids" by Alfie Kohn (2010), and she responded with a blog post that pushed back against his ideas by citing the realities of the classroom (Smith, 2010a). As many bloggers do, Anne then tweeted a link to her blog post, inviting others to come and read and share their thoughts. Sure enough, Kohn read the tweet, read her blog post, and then exchanged emails with her to help clarify his points and offer suggestions that she might try in her classroom. Naturally, this all led to an extended conversation with her students not only about the power of the connections, but also about how they could improve their classroom experience in meaningful ways (Smith, 2010b).

Finally, last fall, Anne invited educators in her network to collaborate with her students in creating "This I Believe" essays and podcasts fashioned after the popular National Public Radio segment. In a blog post, she wrote:

> I want my students to benefit not only from knowing what their peers believe, or what the other AHS classes believe, but to hear and see what the world values. What do kids elsewhere in the U.S. believe in? What do kids elsewhere in the world believe in? What do some of the learned professionals that I know believe in? I want my students to walk away from this experience realizing the power they have as professional writers as well as connecting to other teenagers and adults from around the world. I want to see them exchange ideas, foster relationships, and appreciate the variety of perspectives. (Smith, 2010c)

She added a link to a simple Google form at http://ahsthisibelieve .wikispaces.com/ where other teachers could sign up to participate in the project, and at this writing, her students are working with almost six hundred students from eight states and three countries.

While there is much to take from Anne's experiences, what's most important is her willingness to be transparent not just about the creative ways she's setting out to create these connections but also about the reflective practice she models on her blog. She encourages her students to read her blog, and they know that she writes about her classroom experiences there. It gives them a great example to follow as they create their own personal learning networks through their participation in class. All students blog, collaborate on wikis, and share their work widely in many different ways.

"The biggest shift for me personally was understanding that teaching now means sharing on a lot of different levels," she says. "You can't just take and not give back; I have to give back. My responsibility as an educator, as a parent and as a human is to give back ideas, to say 'here are my ideas, what are yours?'"

That type of participation and "giving back" is foundational when it comes to effective, successful networked classrooms. It's an ethos that is felt by everyone in the classroom community—students and teachers alike. Succeeding in a networked learning world is all about participating, and the more opportunities we can give our students to interact with those global audiences, the better.

Brian Crosby

Trying to help students see these connections when they don't have a great deal of Internet access outside the classroom to begin with is more difficult but still possible. In Brian Crosby's case, while the technological barriers for most of his fifth-grade students in Sparks, Nevada, are pretty high, networking within the classroom and the school are still powerful ways of getting kids to see the potentials of online networks.

To get a clear sense of the poverty in which most of Brian's students find themselves, you might want to take a few minutes to watch this TED talk that he gave in Denver in 2010: www.youtube.com/watch?v=66mrAzz7nLw (TEDxTalks, 2010a). Ninety percent of his students qualify for free lunch, and only about half of his students in 2010 knew what state they lived in. Only three knew what country. Obviously, it's a difficult starting point for a discussion of learning networks with his students, but Brian, who has been blogging away at *Learning Is Messy* (www.learningismessy.com) for over four years, isn't daunted.

"It's important that students know they can network in their schools, that they have access to the math teacher down the hall and the science teacher and others in the community," Brian says. "But any chance we have to show them those networks extend beyond the classroom walls, we need to take advantage of it" (B. Crosby, personal communication, November 5, 2010).

That can be as simple as bringing kids who are home with illnesses into the classroom via Skype. A few years ago, Brian was told that he had a new student in his class, but that she was unable to come to school because she had leukemia. Instead of simply receiving packets of work to complete at home, Celeste joined her classmates every day through a laptop setup on the desk where she would normally have been sitting. The Skype video feature let her see the other students, while they could see her as well. She could hear Brian's lessons and participate in the discussions, and over time, she became just another student in the class. In the interest of sharing, Brian made a video of the experience (www.arisleyschool.org/Inclusion .mov), which has been viewed over half a million times at this writing.

That idea of making virtual students a part of the physical space holds true even for students 2,500 miles away. When Brian's classes collaborated with Long Island teacher Lisa Parisi's students on a project based on the book *The Mysteries of Harris Burdick* by Chris Van Allsburg, he soon found himself teaching her kids and vice versa.

"When you do collaborations of this type, you find your classroom expanding in interesting ways," he says. "You find you're helping to mentor a whole group of kids that you'll never meet, and that can have some unexpected benefits for everyone."

The Harris Burdick project is another great example of using networked spaces to expand the students' sense of the classroom as well. For those unfamiliar with the book, it offers a series of enigmatic drawings for which the accompanying story has supposedly been lost. Readers have the chance then to create their own new narratives around the pictures. Brian and Lisa's students formed small groups, two from each classroom for each drawing, and embarked on a process of writing these new stories. They used Google Docs to create the outlines and compose their stories asynchronously (which was important, considering the three-hour time difference). Toward the end of the process, they shifted their schedules to allow the groups to meet synchronously using Skype, editing their Google Docs and discussing those edits in real time. In Brian's words, that's when the magic really began.

None of the magic would have happened at all, however, if both Brian and Lisa hadn't already been growing their own learning networks and connections. They originally connected their classes while using Classblogmeister, a blogging tool specifically made for school use, and they had their students reading and commenting on each others' posts. Then they also connected on Twitter, and through their interactions there, they started working on the book collaboration separately. Because both had existing networks, they were able to expand the project to include more than a dozen other classes from across the United States and as far away as Perth, Australia. The results, to put it mildly, were impressive and were published on a culminating wiki for the world to see.

Since then, Brian has been looking for more and more ways to bring the world into his classroom, and a quick glance at his wiki speaks volumes about those efforts. His kids have sent "high hopes" up into the air on a weather balloon along with the hopes they collected from dozens of other classrooms around the world. They've gone "Around the World in 80 Days," Skyping into classrooms in Argentina, Thailand, Iceland, New Zealand, and Canada. They've made public service announcements for the City of Reno, and they've hosted a slew of experts and leaders both in and out of the classroom. Almost everything they do extends their connections.

"I'm networked with other teachers and experts, and my kids are, too," Brian says. "My kids especially know so little about the world that networking the classroom like this is a priority, even though we don't have a great deal of technology either in the classroom, or in my students' case, outside the classroom. We just make it happen."

Shannon Miller

Even educators who haven't been participating in networked learning spaces for very long are finding ways to make their classroom walls a little thinner. In some cases, they're tearing the walls down. Shannon Miller—a teacher-librarian/technology coordinator for the Van Meter, Iowa, school district—went from starting to find her own connections in 2009 to teaching a full-fledged personal learning networks course for students in 2010. The results, both for her own learning and for that of her students, have been pretty impressive.

"We're literally in the middle of a cornfield," Shannon says, "and as I started making my own connections in the world, I also started thinking 'why can't we create a class to get our kids connecting in these ways as well'" (S. Miller, personal communication, November 11, 2010).

Since connections are the focus of the curriculum, Shannon spends the first half of the eighteen-week class doing just that, finding other classrooms and other teachers to connect her students with. She tries to do so in a way that both sides gain value. For instance, on a regular basis, her students learn how to use different Web 2.0 tools from the tool creators themselves as they Skype into her classroom. In return, her students give the developers feedback on what's working and what's not. If you're using tools like Juxio, Pixton, Diigo, or many others, odds are the students at Van Meter have had a hand in what you're doing. Shannon uses the interactions as a way for them to learn not just about the tools but about how the tools are created.

In addition, in 2010 she connected with Bill Brannick, the principal of Archbishop Pendergrast High School in Philadelphia; before long, Shannon's class had doubled in size as she began to teach his students virtually as well. Not long after, Patrick Larkin, a principal in Burlington, Massachusetts, added some of his students to the mix. Students in all of the classes connect through a variety of tools from social bookmarking to RSS feeds to Skype to Twitter, and they comment on each other's blogs and work collaboratively on projects. To make it all work, Shannon keeps all of her lesson plans on an open Google Calendar where anyone can follow along (Miller, 2010b). (Visit **go.solution-tree.com/technology** for a link to this calendar.)

Much of the early course curriculum is focused on the nuances of creating these learning networks and the tools required. The syllabus covers an impressive array:

> Students will become familiar with and use social networking tools, such as: Blogs, Wikis, Nings, Twitter, RSS Feeds (Google Reader), Diigo and Diigolet, YouTube, Foursquare, LinkedIn, Skype, Flickr, Facebook, Shelfari/Good Books, uStream, as well as Web 2.0 tools, such as: photo and slideshow creators, digital storytelling tools, comic and second life tools, interactive presentation tools, graphic and personal organizers, movie creators, photo tools, timeline creators, comic creators, music/sound tools, app inventors, poster creators, along with others. Students will also learn how to use a variety of tools to assist with online learning such as conversion tools, backchanneling tools, and others. Students will also learn about GoDaddy.com and the possibility of their own domain. (Miller, 2010a)

Ultimately, the personal learning networks class is about how to use those tools to build connections. On their blogs, students reflect often on how they go about finding people to learn with, the ethics and responsibilities that go along with that work, and how they are being effective in their pursuits. They talk in depth about how to use Twitter, for instance, not only to share with others but to promote their own work, which they share on their blogs. That, in turn, leads to conversations about "digital footprints" and rigor in the process, and as a classroom community, the work is about how to support those efforts at every turn. It's an important foundation as, in the second half, Shannon gives her students more responsibility to begin creating their own connections and self-direct their learning.

"For some kids, it's all about getting over the fear of being embarrassed or of doing something wrong when they share their work online," Shannon says. "We do a lot of sharing inside the classroom first to really give the kids the confidence to start putting stuff out there more widely online."

Assessment is a challenge, especially in a district that is moving toward standards-based grading. But much of it is based on the students' own sense of what the class has taught them. Shannon believes the important question for students to think deeply about is "How has this changed my thinking/perspective of the world?" It's a reflection process that students engage in on a regular basis.

There's an irony to all of this work, however, and Shannon knows it. At the end of the day, networking shouldn't really be a "course" at all; it should simply be a part of how we do learning in schools today. She sees the course as a necessary first step, however—not just for her students, but for her colleagues as well.

"Right now, over half of our classrooms at Van Meter are connecting to someone somewhere else; they're on the road to being networked," she says. "I think much of that is because this class gives us the opportunity to show what's possible. This is exciting; our kids demand this because this is their world. And when they start sharing their expertise around these ideas in other classrooms with other teachers, those teachers get interested and the concepts grow. We're not at a point yet where these skills are being taught K–12, but we're definitely moving in that direction."

In many ways, teaching the personal learning networks course has been almost as transformative for Shannon as her own personal learning experiences online.

"I've never felt smarter in my life," she says. "I have a masters and two other degrees and yet I've never learned more than in the last year. A lot of people find it overwhelming and wonder how to make time for it, but you just have to find your own groove with how you use it, and when you do, the connections add so much to your life."

Strategies for the Networked Classroom

No question, these stories are in many ways exceptional, and we hope they begin to show the potential shift that networked-based curricula and pedagogies create in the classroom. While these kinds of experiences do require a certain amount of technology knowledge and Internet access, even more they require a shift in practice and thinking. As teachers, Anne, Brian, and Shannon (and many others we wish we could highlight here) have not only come to know the power of networked learning in their lives but also to understand the critical need for students to experience that power in their own learning lives as well. Because of these teachers' commitment to learning in these contexts, their students are reaping the benefits.

When we look at what these teachers and their students are doing in these projects, we notice a fairly narrow range of five methods for using networked learning spaces online in classrooms:

1. Connect students and teachers inside the classroom.

2. Publish student and teacher work locally and globally.

3. Connect students and teachers outside the classroom.

4. Connect with experts around the world.

5. Collaborate with others to create and share knowledge.

Very few teachers employ more than one or two of these strategies currently, but the most effective networked classrooms have a healthy mix of all five. In other words, networked classrooms have a culture of connections in which both teachers and students learn, and there is an expectation that the classroom experience will regularly reach far beyond the four walls. In addition, safety, balance, and ethics become an integral part of those interactions, not something that is taught in isolation.

While we don't offer this list of five strategies as a continuum per se, we can see them as a part of a "thin walls" construction process that starts with local connections, moves to global publishing, and then grows into extended connections, collaborations, and network building. Each step can serve as a building block for the next, moving students and teachers toward a fundamental shift in the way they see their classrooms and their roles in them. Let's take a moment to break down each of these and see how we might make them work.

Connect Students and Teachers Inside the Classroom

Creating connections inside the classroom is an important first step, and as Shannon's story shows, it gives teachers a chance to lay the groundwork for opening up the classroom later. In some ways, it's a way to "sandbox" the basic skills and literacies that kids will need to know in their more global interactions. While there are many ways to do this, one easy way is to create either classroom or individual blogs that are private or password protected. Teachers often start with just one blog that students can post to or comment on in order to learn and practice the rules of the road, so to speak, eventually giving them the opportunity to start their own blogs. Some great options for doing just that are www.21classes.com, www

.edublogs.org, or www.classblogmeister.com. These sites make it fairly easy to limit the audience and allow for drafting and thinking to be done in private. All content on these sites can be easily moderated by teachers, and there are easy options to open posts to larger audiences when the class is ready.

Other tools teachers use to connect students in the classroom are chat or backchannel sites such as www.todaysmeet.com or www.coveritlive .com, which allow them to interact with one another using text in an online space while watching a presentation or a lesson. In addition, private wikis are a click away at www.wikispaces.com or www.pbworks .com, sites where students can begin collaborating with one another to collect resources or share projects. There are even opportunities to create classroom social network sites using tools like www.edmodo.com or www .ning.com. In both cases, members can use the space to create and share content, link to resources on the web, and add their own videos, photos, and more. (Visit **go.solution-tree.com/technology** to access live versions of all links.)

Publish Student and Teacher Work Locally and Globally

Publishing can take many forms and should be seen as a necessary step to creating the global connections that build learning networks even if there isn't a lot of commenting or interaction at the outset. In many cases, what's published could be artifacts of learning from the classroom, projects, essays, artwork, and more. While personal blogs could (and perhaps should) be considered in the mix, we're talking here about work that may go beyond written texts. A public blog could serve as a great publishing vehicle for these types of multimedia artifacts.

While the different tools teachers and students are using number in the hundreds (at least), we'll quickly suggest some of the most popular publishing sites for students of all ages. To publish photos, try www.flickr.com or www.photobucket.com; both are places where you can create private and public spaces for student work. Creating video? Both www.youtube.com, or if that's blocked, www.teachertube.com will allow uploads for free. Screencasts—videos of what you are doing on your computer screen with a voice-over—can be captured with tools like www.jingproject.com or www .screentoaster.com. You can upload student PowerPoint-like presentations at www.slideshare.com. And if you create podcasts (audio stories or narratives using Audacity), you can share those at www.audioboo.com or even www.posterous.com.

Connect Students and Teachers Outside the Classroom

Connecting outside the classroom should be a logical outgrowth of the publishing you and your students do. Publishing is what makes you findable to others who are just a Google search away. Whether it's other classrooms or other expert mentors, and whether it's solicited or happens by chance, the goal of publishing should be to make connections around the world, to find others who share an interest or a passion in whatever the topic may be, and to begin to explore the ways in which those others may enhance the learning process. This requires a fair amount of the skills we discussed in chapter 2.

As we see in the previous stories, some of those connections happen by design and others happen serendipitously. Sometimes, these teachers work with nodes already in their networks, so to speak, while other times, teachers and classrooms may just show up at their door. They may also solicit input from "strangers" as well. In some cases, teachers may use their personal Facebook networks to find other classrooms to work with. That's exactly the way these connections work in the real world outside of school, so the more we can model them inside the walls, the better. Teachers might find these new connections at sites like www.classroom20.com, which is a large network of teachers sharing ideas and asking questions, or even http://twitter4teachers.pbworks.com, where you can find listings of educators on Twitter broken down by grade and discipline (among other categories.)

Connect With Experts Around the World

While other teachers and students from around the world can add a lot of learning to your classroom, inviting experts on particular subjects or experiences can have an even greater effect. One early example comes from Will's Modern American Literature class way back in 2003, when he connected with Sue Monk Kidd, the author of *A Secret Life of Bees*, which his students were reading in class. As his students read the novel and shared their thoughts on a class blog, the author followed along and then wrote a 2,300-word reflection that she posted to the class's site. She provided insights and anecdotes about the origins of the story and the writing of the book that had never before been made public.

Other classrooms around the world have brought in scientists from Antarctica, Holocaust historians, poets, and even astronauts on the space shuttle. In many cases, these experts are sharing blogs with students, but more and more, they are making live, virtual appearances using tools such as Skype. (In fact, Skype has developed a site where teachers can connect to experts—and other classrooms—at http://education.skype.com.)

When it comes to working with experts, the best approach is straight-forward. We find that most people are happy to take a moment out of their busy lives to inspire or teach young people. We've seen schools work with authors, journalists, lawyers, scientists, and many other professionals. Many experts whom you might invite into your classrooms are as close as a Google search and an email away. Be polite and keep their commitment small, but meaningful—at least at first. The worst they can say is no, right?

Collaborate With Others to Create and Share Knowledge

Collaborating with others to create meaningful, important work should be the end goal of all this. In fact, we like the way author Clay Shirky suggests that "collective action"—working with others to affect positive change in the world—may be the greatest aspiration of all our connections (Shirky, 2008, Kindle location 47). Obviously, those types of collaborations take more work and planning on the part of both the teacher and the student, but it can be good, important work that gives our kids a sense of what's possible these days.

Aside from using wikis to plan, Skype to communicate, and blogs to bring their work to the world (as well as many other tools), we've seen a number of teachers—working with older kids—beginning to use Facebook groups or www.ning.com sites to bring their collective action to the world. To be sure, simply bringing students together to create resources that add to the global knowledge base is a valuable undertaking, but bringing them together to work as a collective to change the world is even better. For example, we know of one high school physical education class that created a Facebook page to help organize the collection of hair from various barber shops and salons to use in the cleanup of the 2010 oil spill in the Gulf of Mexico. In the process, students learned not just about the environmental issues surrounding the spill but how to more effectively organize online. With the global reach that we now have, all it takes is a bit of creativity and coordination to make the world a better place. To that end, we hope you'll keep in mind the larger potentials of the networked classroom by always asking, "What can my students create and share with the world that might lead to positive social change or opportunities for others to learn?" It's not just about individuals adding value; all of us are better than one of us.

The more you become a networked learner, the less daunting this will become from a how-to-do-it standpoint. We know there are many other considerations here, like safety, access, and others that we'll be addressing both later in this chapter and the next. The bottom line is this: these types of interactions in the classroom must be standard fare if we are to create literate readers and writers and if we are going to help students understand how to create their own learning opportunities.

The Challenges of the Networked Classroom

For all of the new opportunities for learning in these connected classrooms, making them work effectively is not without speed bumps. There's no substitute for having extensive practical experience in your personal learning to draw upon when attempting to meet the challenges head on. While we feel that none of these are insurmountable in and of themselves, we also understand that opening up the classroom in the ways we've been describing will create some additional challenges. To help make sense of them, here's a partial list of considerations that will most likely require some consideration:

- Safety and ethical use

- Transparency

- Assessment

- Ownership and rights

- Parents

Safety and Ethical Use

No question, the safety of every student is paramount as we begin to help kids fashion and connect to their own learning networks online. Just as in life offline, there are dangers in our online interactions, but the opportunities for positive, powerful learning interactions far outweigh the risks. In many ways, we have been "Datelined" to death into believing there is a predator around every corner on the Internet. We don't mean to minimize the seriousness of this discussion in any way, but the reality is that our kids are still much more likely to be preyed on by people in their physical spaces—people they know in real life—than by strangers online. As a task force created by forty-nine state attorneys general found in 2009, the problem of sexual solicitation of children online is "not a significant problem" (Stone, 2009).

Similarly, ethical use of the web is an important part of participating in online networks. With access to so much information and content and so many ways to interact, it's becoming easier and easier to cheat, plagiarize, or use the web as a medium for abuse and bullying. In fact, many teachers tell us one of the reasons they stay off the web is because of the highly confrontational nature of many discussion boards or comment threads online. While there's no doubt that online debates can become negative, the vast majority of online interactions are appropriate and helpful.

When bad things do happen online, the news is never good, and it makes headlines far and wide. At this writing, in fact, we're only weeks removed from the suicide of a Rutgers University student, "outed" by his roommates who secretly live-streamed a sexual encounter from his dorm room. The story was a sobering reminder of what can go wrong, but it also underscores the need for online behavior instruction in our schools. Just as we teach our kids how to make smart decisions when they get behind the wheel of a car, we have to teach our kids how to drive on the web as well. They have to know that almost all of the rules that apply in face-to-face conversation apply online, too.

The safe and ethical use of online spaces can't be taught in an isolated unit in the curriculum. Nor can it be taught in a two-hour presentation by a retired police officer or an FBI agent. Part of the safety discussion has to center around the extent to which we allow students and teachers to use social spaces in the classroom. All too often, we've seen districts equate keeping students safe with filtering any online access to people and to content that hasn't been created in traditional ways (blogs, Wikipedia, YouTube, and so on). Even worse, many districts do not give teachers the ability to override the filter at their desktops or laptops if they find blocked sites that they deign either appropriate or relevant to the curriculum. In our view, that strategy actually makes students *less* safe. Students go home to primarily unfiltered access without having first learned, in the critical classroom context, how to make good choices about the content and people they connect with. Additionally, it conveys a lack of professional respect to adult teachers in those classrooms.

Safety is more than just a change in district policy, obviously. It's not something we can teach as a unit or add on to the curriculum, either. Web safety and ethical use should simply be a part of our operating culture in schools. In every grade and in every classroom, students should be seeing adults making smart decisions in their own online practice as a daily occurrence. We may need to revise our current acceptable-use policies to clearly define our expectations for participating in networked interactions to students and their parents, as well as the consequences for irresponsible use. (More on that in chapter 5.) These are teachable moments: opportunities to deepen the understanding of our students regarding how to use the web appropriately in real, uncontrived ways.

A case in point: when the Science Leadership Academy (SLA) opened in Philadelphia in 2006, the initial freshman class experienced an outbreak of online bullying from some students using the instant messaging (IM) client on the school-provided computers. Not only was the bullying abusive to students, it was disruptive to the classroom practice of SLA teachers. Unlike most schools, which probably would have simply shut down access to chatting at that point, the school chose to use the bad behavior as an opportunity to teach students about the consequences of the bullying and to discuss more appropriate practice.

"Our kids are going to have to use social media tools like IM in their adult, professional lives," says SLA principal Chris Lehmann. "Just making it go away isn't going to solve the problem. We felt that it was up to the school to take the issue seriously when it was brought to us, to work with the kids to teach them why cyber-bullying was not o.k., and to help them develop strategies for dealing with it when they encountered it" (C. Lehmann, personal communication, January 8, 2011).

Students and teachers joined for schoolwide meetings to discuss the problem, with those being bullied sharing their feelings and teachers sharing the effects it was having on the school. Immediately afterward, things improved, and students actually formed strategies on their own to quickly block those students who continued to try to misuse the technology. Today IM is a valuable part of the culture of learning at the school.

"All of this speaks to the need to help students become better citizens," says Chris, "and in this age, that must include cyber-citizenship."

Transparency

We noted earlier that transparency brings great value to the learning interaction. It's also a challenge, however, as it's difficult for many to open up their classrooms and, to some extent, their students to the world online. Often, the transparency of the networked classroom is initially uncomfortable, but it's necessary for making those connections happen. Transparency can take many forms, depending on the comfort level of the district, the teacher, and the general school community. We've seen any number of variations. At the most transparent end of the spectrum are classrooms like the live-streamed classroom of fifth-grade teacher William Chamberlain at Noel Elementary School in Missouri. Anyone can hop over to *Mr. C's Class Blog* (http://mrcsclassblog.blogspot.com) and watch what's going on in his classroom at any time during the day. In addition, readers can find all sorts of other links to student projects, blog posts, videos, and more. It's easy to find comments on the site from places like the Melville Intermediate School in New Zealand and a host of other schools around the world, as well as a list of global student blogs that William's own students read on a regular basis.

"For me and my students it is about being part of a larger community; it's a constant reminder of the world outside our classroom," William says. "My students quickly come to realize our world is literally an Internet connection away" (W. Chamberlain, personal communication, November 4, 2010).

Other classrooms may not be as transparent as his, but there are many examples of students blogging to the world, producing podcasts, and working collaboratively in public with students in other parts of the globe. Take, for instance, kindergarten teacher Maria Knee's blog (http://classblogmeister.com /blog.php?blogger_id=51141), whose tagline reads "We want to share our work with our families and the world." She regularly posts videos of classroom happenings as well as student art and writing, many of which get comments from other teachers and classrooms from around the world.

To meet the challenges of transparency, everyone—students, parents, teachers, and administrators—needs to be on the same page regarding the benefits of sharing work online. In addition to that responsible-use policy we've already mentioned, we need to be clear with those participating exactly how open we intend these spaces to be and why. The *why* question, as always, is best answered by a teacher-learner who has participated in these spaces already and clearly understands the potentials and pitfalls.

Assessment

If we teach these network-building skills to our students in the classroom, how do we begin to assess their literacy in these areas and others? We've never really taught these types of skills in the past, and we struggle with knowing exactly what to assess. Obviously, it's not as easy as making sure our students can write in grammatically correct sentences. In addition, assessing how well students make connections with other teachers and learners around the globe doesn't lend itself easily to standardization. In other words, we don't see assessment of network-building skills as a unit test but instead as an ongoing formative assessment as these skills develop over time.

Many teachers attempt to quantify the participation of their students in networked spaces by giving grades based on the number of blog posts or comments. While those types of assessments may serve some role, we'd advocate for a more qualitative strategy. Any assessment of networked learning should include a healthy amount of self-reflection on the part of the student. That reflection may be given through oral conferences, written responses (perhaps on a blog post), or open classroom discussion about the process. In all of this, it's imperative that the teacher share reflections on his or her own process with the class, sharing successes as well as struggles that might be addressed by the experiences of others.

While a quick Google search for "assessing 21st century learning" will land quite a few results, we want to highlight the approach taken by Clarence Fisher, whom you met earlier in this chapter. In 2010, Clarence created what he calls a "Connecting Assessment" rubric that he uses with his students to get a clear sense of what their participation looks like and how successful they are at creating networked connections. (Visit **go.solution -tree.com/technology** for a link to this rubric.) He describes the rubric as a "conversation starter with students" that they can use in small groups to discuss their practice or as a self-reflection. As you look at it, remember that this is for a middle school class, but it could easily be modified for older or younger students (Fisher, n. d.).

This rubric gives students a clear sense of both the expectations for their participation and the opportunity to meaningfully practice their skills. For instance, in the "Developing a Global Understanding" section, students are expected to "access content from at least three different continents" on a regular basis and to regularly create content about global issues as well. In the "Connecting and Networking" portion, Clarence expects students to be constantly revising and reflecting on their information flows and the ways in which they interact with others outside the classroom. Finally, the checklist at the end of the rubric provides students with quick reminders as to the types of habits they should be establishing in order to build their networking skills effectively.

Certainly, there are many ways to begin assessing these types of outcomes. The focus, however, should not be on whether or not a student can successfully use a particular tool to make something but instead on whether that student knows how to make that blog post or YouTube video or SlideShare presentation *connect to others* with whom she can potentially learn more. The goal is not sharing for the sake of sharing; it's sharing for the sake of connecting and learning. That's the important piece for us to assess and to ensure that our students can do well.

Ownership and Rights

At a time when so many people are sharing so much content online, using that content in ways that might not be ethically or even legally appropriate has never been easier. This presents a number of complex issues surrounding the ways we and our students navigate these online spaces and create and share work with the world. Most importantly, as educators begin to be more transparent about their own practices, it's imperative that we engage in ongoing conversations about how things are changing and model appropriate use.

Again, none of these discussions or practices should be added to the current curriculum as a unit. We need to be talking about copyright even with first and second graders as we help them build the skills to create their own online portfolios. Too often we've seen a haphazard approach to instilling a culture of ethical and appropriate use—an approach built more on policy and punishments than real-world application in the classroom. Because these concepts are in flux, parents have to be educated as well in hopes of getting them to partner with us in the process.

At a time when collaborative online workspaces are popping up almost daily, perhaps the most pressing need is for a professional discussion about what we should expect of students. For example, www.dweeber .com is a site used by students to do homework together, tutor one another, and share all sorts of information. It's a place where kids can go to make positive connections, but many teachers see it and other sites or tools like it (Facebook groups or even IM or Skype) as vehicles for cheating—for working together when the expectation is that students will work alone. This too is changing, however. Denmark, for example, recently allowed students to access the web during final exams (Hobson, 2009). In a world where we can collaborate so easily online, do we need to change our thinking or expectations about student work? Is there a new line to be drawn in terms of "doing your own work" as opposed to tapping into the wisdom of the network to find answers and create solutions? It's a question that has no easy answer, and one worth a deep discussion within every school community.

We urge every educator to take a look at Creative Commons (http://cre ativecommons.org), a site on which creators of photos, music, videos and more can assign legally binding copyrights to their online work to make it easier for others to use. Right now, in the United States at least, it's difficult to use copyrighted works because of the permissions involved. (In our opinion, the idea that works take eighty years after the death of the creator to fall into the public domain to be exceptionally onerous.) At Creative Commons, we can find work that is licensed to use with simple attribution to the author or by allowing the material to be used for any noncommercial purposes. In addition, we can have our students choose licenses for their own original published work while engaging them in a conversation about what copyright means and what the implications are for not abiding by it.

Parents

Parents aren't necessarily a challenge to changing your classroom per se, but they are an important constituency that's always better to have with you than against you. To that end, we suggest being as communicative as possible with them in explaining the changes you're trying to effect with your students. No doubt parents (as well as department supervisors, principals, board members, and others) will want to know how your uses of learning networks with your students will help them reach the goals and objectives of the curriculum and achieve at a higher level. If you can't connect those dots, this will be difficult work indeed. And, obviously, you must be able to articulate how students will be kept safe in the classroom while interacting in these global ways. You'll have a leg up in that conversation if you can point to your own experiences online as a foundation for your pedagogy.

As much as you can, give parents a chance to be a part of the learning networks you create with your students. When appropriate, you might ask them to comment on blog posts, participate in Skype conversations, or even log in to a backchannel conversation while watching a live stream of a classroom event. If you can, give them copies of the books your students are reading in class, and set them up with their own book club blog where they can read along and participate. Have your students create screencast tutorials for parents and post them on a class wiki for easy access. With a little creative thinking, it's not hard to bring parents into the mix. In all honesty, it's an important part of the larger goal of building support for change across your school—a topic we'll discuss much more in chapters 4 and 5.

Making the Move

We know that for many, this move to a more networked classroom seems huge, and it is. As we said before, in its ultimate form, this move changes the role of the teacher and the notion of what learning looks like in schools. Walking by any of the classrooms in this chapter's vignettes, you'd see students working independently, driving their own learning, with their teachers learning alongside them. There's little paper being passed back and forth, very little homework in the traditional sense, and the role of the instructor is more that of a coach or facilitator than an all-knowing expert who delivers the curriculum. While those may seem like huge shifts, they are really grounded in much smaller ones that begin by simply thinking differently about small parts of the curriculum that already exist, not throwing it all out and starting from scratch.

Author Sheryl Nussbaum-Beach, who is also the cofounder with Will of Powerful Learning Practice (www.plpnetwork.com), talks about these smaller shifts when she advocates for "21st Century-izing" your current lesson plans (S. Nussbaum-Beach, personal communication, November 12, 2010). In effect, she advocates taking what you already do well in the classroom and simply re-envisioning it through more of a 21st century lens, one that hopefully you've developed through your own participation in the network. For instance, say one of the most effective aspects of your current classroom is the role-playing activity your students do to more deeply understand the characters in a book they are reading. Right now, most teachers who use role play have their students engage in discussions or debates inside the classroom, during the class period, with a limited audience. But what if you were to connect your classroom to another classroom from another part of the globe and have your students discuss and debate in the same way in an online setting? It could be through regular blog posts in character, a live Skype debate, or even a live-streamed event to the world using Ustream (www.ustream.tv). In this way, students could still show their understanding of the characters, but they would also begin to understand and build connections outside the classroom. You might also give students options as to how they want to publish and share their understanding of the characters: a short YouTube video, a multimedia poster at Glogster (www.glogster.com), or a photo story at VoiceThread (http://voicethread.com). By giving students a choice of tools to use to show their knowledge, you give them more ownership over the learning process. (Visit **go.solution-tree.com/technology** for live versions of all links.)

In other words, *you can do this.*

We'll leave you with some reminders and helpful hints in terms of starting your own networked learning space:

- **It starts with you.** As always, having your own personal contexts for these types of interactions is imperative for helping your students experience the potentials themselves.

- **Start small.** Let the connections happen locally first, within the four walls, and then begin to think of easy ways to bring the outside world in.

- **Embrace uncertainty and failure.** This is different from what you've been doing. It won't be smooth sailing 100 percent of the time. That's OK.

- **Model, model, model.** Be transparent about your own learning in these contexts. Reflect with your students and colleagues on a regular basis, and share your best practices to your networks and communities online.

- **Remember the goal.** Very few adults are engaged in teaching these networking literacies to kids right now. Students need our help to create their own learning opportunities online.

If you're looking for a role model in this transition, we'd suggest Shelley Wright, a high school teacher from Moose Jaw, Saskatchewan, who started this journey for herself last fall. Her blog, *Wright'sRoom* (http://shelleywright .wordpress.com), has chronicled her experiences in an inspiring way, and it speaks eloquently to all of the themes we've offered here. In one particularly moving excerpt, Shelley talks about the difficulty of this shift:

> Normally, in beginning a unit on Civil Rights, I would be the Civil Rights expert, and would have spent several days lecturing and telling stories of the great heroes of the movement. We would have spent time talking, discussing the issues, and laughing. I would be connected with my class. But today, I was not.
>
> Today, instead of teaching them information, I was teaching them how to learn. And yet, I'm not sure what my new role in this is. I'm not sure how to connect to my students and their learning process while doing this. I'm not sure how to laugh and enjoy them. And I was not expecting the profound sense of loss and the pain accompanying it. (Wright, 2010a)

But just a few weeks later, she wrote:

> This, in many ways, was a great week. Everything has changed in my classroom, and until the end of the semester, I will be teaching my students to learn and problem solve, rather than content. The ironic thing is, I have tried this in my classroom before; however, I always felt like I wasn't doing my job, and so I quickly reverted back to the old way. After all, wasn't I hired to teach them? But as Oscar Wilde eloquently quipped, "nothing that is worth learning can be taught."
>
> For me, this is just the beginning. Two of my classes this semester are being connected with e-pals half-way across the world. They're really excited about this, as am I. My ELA 20 class is going to spend several weeks learning in our own version of the TED-X Classroom Project . . .
>
> It seems in the past two months that everything has changed. I can't imagine going back to running my classroom as I used [to]; Thankfully, I don't have to. (Wright, 2010b)

May your own learning journey be as profound and important as Shelley's.

CHAPTER 4

BECOMING A NETWORKED SCHOOL

On the opening day of the 2009 school year, Superintendent Lisa Brady stood in front of the 250 teachers at Hunterdon Central Regional High School in Flemington, New Jersey, and started a new conversation about learning in her district. "Our students are entering a different world," Lisa said, "one that is more global, more connected, more diverse and less structured than the one we knew. Our students are going to change jobs more often than we did, sometimes changing their field as well. To be prepared, they will need the skills that we have always taught, like the ability to write effectively, speak confidently, and think critically, but now they will also need skills that we have not always emphasized, like the ability to solve open-ended complex problems using creative approaches and to collaborate with peers around the world. Most likely, they'll need to learn 'on the fly' every day of their lives" (L. Brady, personal communication, September 8, 2009).

What Lisa said next is important for all of us to hear. "I only know two things for sure about the situation that faces us right now as educators," she said. "The first is that we will need to do things differently than we have done them before, teaching in new ways, with new methods of learning using new technologies in our classrooms. The second is that the best path to those changes isn't clear right now, and we will need every member of this community to work together to figure it out. Let me be clear about this—I need your ideas, your energy, your caring for our kids, and, most of all, I need your leadership."

Our Kids Need Everyone

Lisa knows that educators are at a critical moment of change that requires us to prepare our students not only to meet the traditional expectations we've had for a hundred years, but also to succeed in this new world of networked learning—a world that is just now emerging and that hasn't yet been captured in state tests or in college entrance exams or even in the larger conversation around education reform. In essence, we face the "problems" and the "challenge" we mentioned before; we've got to change, even though the way to change isn't clear and no one is demanding us to do so. Every school needs to figure out a solution, and every educator needs to start learning about networks so they can help develop that solution.

Each member of your school must participate if you are going to deliver what students need to succeed. It's one thing if an individual teacher employs PLNs in the classes that she teaches, but it's another thing entirely if everyone in the school is engaged in the practice. It changes not only the goals that we have for students but the school culture as well. It's the difference between learning and "learning how to learn." In an ideal world, students won't graduate with a bunch of tattered books and notes in three-ring binders; they will graduate with a global network of connections they can take with them to college or work, expanding it, growing it every day of their lives.

There are at least two other reasons your entire school should engage in this work. First, it gets easier for every teacher to change his or her classroom when similar changes are taking place throughout the school. Our schools are places of habit, and it is difficult to disrupt the normal routines, some of which have continued unabated for over one hundred years. When we introduce learning networks into our curriculum and instruction, there is a period of adjustment that students (and sometimes parents) will need to undergo to think of this as "learning." This adjustment period passes much more quickly if students are immersed in the process of connecting in several classes at once. At the end of the day, networked learning is not a unit that we add on to the seventh-grade English class. Instead, these skills and literacies should be clearly articulated throughout the K–12 curriculum so that first graders, for instance, might be blogging with their peers while juniors in a high school science section might be creating collaborative videos with a classroom half a world away. In other words, the curriculum as a whole should provide a clear path for teachers to scaffold the safe, effective, and ethical use of these technologies for learning into everyday classroom life.

Second, if educators fail to participate in these networks, it will hurt not only their personal professional growth but the learning of the entire community. Learning in networks is the air and water of 21st century learning. While there are many opportunities to learn offline—individual study, conferences, and so on—these experiences are magnified significantly when combined with daily discussion with colleagues from around the world. These networks will energize your school with ideas for lesson plans, remediation, assessment, homework, instructional techniques, and dozens of other things that educators want to know. The full community needs to participate to collect and share as many of these ideas as possible if the school intends to deliver the best education.

As we've seen, it's challenging but possible to become networked learners and, in turn, to create global classrooms. We see those changes happening daily. But shifting to become networked on the school level is harder. In fact, few existing schools have gone very far down this path in planned, systemic ways. For those that have started, however, the work has proven among the most exciting they have ever done. It will take years. It will take commitment. But it's a rewarding shift that enables us to serve our students and our communities more effectively.

Fortunately, there is a path to changing your school that is manageable in both time and effort. In this chapter and the next, we're going to help you get on that path. In this chapter, we focus on your people—detailing what you need to do to bring your adults into the world of networked learning in a structured way that ensures success. Then we'll build on that foundation in chapter 5, talking about the major considerations you'll need to work through—money, policies, technology, and resistance—in order to bring it all to your students in a cohesive, meaningful way.

Making Change: The Three Cornerstones

Let's start with a step-by-step process for laying the groundwork that will enable every teacher in your school to build his or her own personal learning network. This process was created from our own work in schools and the work of other educators and was informed by the literature of change management and project planning. It calls for three foundational parts that you will need to build over the course of a year. We like to call these (1) the compelling case, (2) the change team, and (3) the pilot. Each is an important cornerstone of the change process, indispensable to whole-school participation in learning networks. Although we've written this chapter from the perspective of a single school, the approach works for any size undertaking—from small departments to a large multischool district.

So what are these three cornerstones, and why are they so important? First, the *compelling case* explains why every member of your school community needs to master networked learning. It's a personalized narrative that answers the question "Why should we change?" Once you have constructed this case, we suggest that you use it to assemble a *change team*. This is a dedicated group of educators who will lead your school through the process of implementing learning networks. Ideally, the team will come from all parts of the school, and team members will have their hands in every part of the process from start to finish. They will be the first to engage with these networks to change their own learning, and they will determine collectively the best way to bring everyone else on board. Finally, the work of the change team will culminate in a *pilot program*, which is the expansion of this work throughout your school. Your pilot will give people beyond the change team an opportunity to practice their use of learning networks, and it will disseminate ideas throughout the school about how networks offer opportunities for new learning.

Many schools try to take a less structured approach to this process. They require teachers to participate in some mandatory professional development around PLNs and then encourage them to use the tools in the classroom. But this informal approach can only take you so far, often resulting in a handful of isolated teachers trying to change their classrooms and, many times, giving up. These three steps ensure that does not happen. With a strong argument for the use of learning networks (the compelling case), a strong group guiding the process (the change team), and a well-planned, well-supported professional development program (the pilot), actual use of the networks is very high. This approach, while a little more time consuming, ensures that teachers will understand networked learning and will apply their new knowledge to their classrooms.

This three-pronged approach will take about a year—a few weeks to develop the compelling case, a few months to work with the change team, and the remaining time to design and begin the launch of the pilot. Of course, spreading these networks effectively throughout every corner of the school will take longer. It should. But your initial foray is manageable—less than 365 days from jotting down your initial thoughts to beginning the spread of networked learning throughout your organization.

One last thing before we get into the details of this work. While it may sound like this chapter is geared toward the traditional "decision makers" within most school systems, it's actually meant for every educator at every level of the school. All of us need to lead at this moment. We have seen the schoolwide adoption of learning networks be initiated by the superintendent, the principal, a veteran teacher, the director of curriculum and instruction, a new teacher, the director of technology, the business officer, and many more. Titles don't really dictate who best grasps this emerging reality, and organizational charts can't show who understands how to learn in networks and who doesn't.

So if you are not the head of your school, you'll need to convince your leadership to undertake this work. In many ways, this is not dissimilar from how your superintendent would need to lay out the rationale for this work to the board or to parents. In both instances, someone (or some group) who understands the power of these networks needs to make a compelling case. So that's where we'll start.

Cornerstone 1: The Compelling Case

In their great book *Switch*, Dan and Chip Heath remind us that the most important aspect of leading change is to explain why (Heath & Heath, 2010). Rest assured, you'll have a lot of folks in your school community asking that question, especially if your school is already successful in the traditional sense. So it's important that you can articulate a compelling case for making these shifts in a short, engaging, heartfelt story that quickly allows the listener to understand the urgency of the task. It's an elevator pitch of sorts, one that appeals to both logic and emotions and invites people into the conversation. If you are the superintendent, this is the case you will use to get resources and support from the board, parents, and teachers. If you are a teacher or staff member, it's the pitch that you (or perhaps a group) will use to convince senior leadership of the importance of using learning networks in and out of the classroom. Either way, it needs to be a convincing, moving story that succinctly lays out exactly why your school should immediately devote the time, energy, and resources to learning in networks.

To help you construct this story, try to answer these three questions:

1. What is the best way to explain how learning networks change the educational landscape to someone in my community who has never heard of one?

2. What are the reasons for adopting learning networks that would drive people in my community to immediate action?

3. What are the pressures that people feel, and how could learning in networks address some of these challenges immediately?

Think of a few sentences that answer each of those questions. Then weave the answers together as a story. The narrative can be told in dozens of ways, but a straightforward approach is to go from the answer to question one, "The reason that learning is changing is . . . ," to question two, "We really need to use learning networks because . . . ," to question three, "Learning networks would solve the problem of . . ." You want to select elements of the story that are clear, solve problems, and empower people in your environment. The story also needs to contain a sense of urgency. Most importantly, you want a story that makes sense to the mind but also touches the heart. This isn't just about arguing an airtight case; it's about making a passionate argument about learning to educators who care about kids.

Obviously, if you've already started creating a PLN for yourself, use it in this work. Connect with people who have already begun to do the work at their schools, sign up for RSS feeds filled with relevant information, and ask questions in your network when you are looking for something or want more help with a point. Often they have already written something for their own school that they would be willing to share. If you are looking for a place to start, try Twitter. Asking for help with the elements of your story can be a terrific way for you to build connections with people online while laying the groundwork for the rest of the school to do the same.

Every school's story will be different, but there are points you can find throughout this book and numerous resources at **go.solution-tree.com /technology**, including examples. Following are some popular elements that appear in many of the stories we have helped schools construct:

- Since the mid-1990s, the sum of human knowledge and two billion potential teachers are available to us online. These shifts have huge implications for the field of education, demanding that we reexamine the way we structure our classrooms and our work with students.

- The ability to easily publish content online and then use this network to connect with people around the world make the web a learning tool of epic proportions, perhaps the most powerful learning tool ever created.

- Educational organizations and publications such as the National Council of Teachers of English, the National Education Technology Plan, *Education Week*, and others are increasingly talking about the importance of learning networks to student learning.

- The ability to tap into outside expertise is a necessary skill for the modern teacher. If she does not learn in this way, it will be impossible for her to stay abreast of her discipline and the larger education conversation.

- Online learning networks are increasingly becoming a fundamental tool in the modern workforce that our students will need to know how to use to compete for jobs in the global marketplace.

- The diversity of views and opinions available in global networks is an essential element to a modern 21st century education. Students not participating in these networks can't really understand the world around them.

- The fact that our students are engaged in social networks is a natural building block for the use of the web for learning, but they need our help to make this critical transition.

- To keep our students safe online, we need to first know how to use these networks ourselves, and we need to teach students how to use them well.

- The web can engage students in the classroom as easily as it engages them outside of it.

- Our professional growth and development as educators is increasingly tied to how connected we are to other educators through these networks effectively and efficiently.

- The only way we can feel in control and save time when facing the avalanche of information in the modern world is to learn how to use learning networks.

- Literacy is now fundamentally tied to our effective use of technology to learn.

Once you've put together your own story, write it down, memorize it, and practice telling it. Bounce it off your friends, and ask them if it makes sense. As world-renowned management consultant Tom Peters suggests,

Sometimes hearing someone else's compelling case can help you build your own. We introduced this chapter by featuring Lisa Brady, superintendent at Hunterdon Central in Flemington, New Jersey, and the 21st century learning work that Central is doing as a community. Lisa and her team have built a compelling case for change at Hunterdon Central by talking about how a high-achieving school district with a reputation of being a challenging academic environment can continue to improve in the 21st century. Here's a glimpse of it in its shortest form.

"Students are entering a rapidly changing, global marketplace in which they will need both old and new skills to compete. Some of these are skills we have always emphasized, like critical thinking and problem solving, but some are skills that we have not traditionally focused on, like entrepreneurship and innovation. To prepare our students to flourish in this fast-changing world, we need to learn the new technologies that are shaping how people learn, and we need to think about how this learning space could be incorporated into our classrooms. At Central we have always taught *lifelong learning* at a very high level, but now that term means something entirely different than it did twenty years ago. As educators, each of us will have to learn in new ways to work together on the evolution of our classrooms for the 21st century."

you want to create the elevator speech that will make people say "wow" (Peters, 1999). In the end, you should be able to make the compelling case for personal learning networks in under three minutes in a way that makes people nod their head in agreement (or at least makes them sit up and take notice). If you are a school leader, repeat the story to your leadership team and some tech-savvy members of your board in an attempt to engage them in a conversation about the importance of this work. If you are a teacher or staff member, make an appointment with someone in leadership and talk through the case. Follow up with some of the videos or short articles that we mention throughout this chapter. As you get feedback, engage others in helping you write the case.

The compelling case is intended to generate agreement about the importance of this work and build enough consensus that your school would be willing to spend some time having a team explore the use of learning networks in more detail. While this is typically easier to initiate if you are the superintendent or principal, it can be done by anyone. We've witnessed it firsthand. Disinterest can quickly change to curiosity simply by sharing relevant examples of how networks can improve teacher and student learning. We have seen it happen over the course of a fifteen-minute video or a ten-minute chat.

As each person becomes convinced, be prepared to answer the question, "What's next?" Your answer? "We build a change team."

Cornerstone 2: The Change Team

If you are going to lead your school in the adoption of learning networks, you can't do it alone. The next critical step in this process is to build a team of leaders for this work. We call this group the change team because that's their purpose: to guide your school through the change process required to ensure learning network use in every classroom and office. John Kotter, a professor at Harvard Business School and world-renowned change expert, makes this one of the first steps of the change process in his best-selling book *Leading Change*. Kotter insists that you need a "powerful guiding coalition," a group of influential people whose power comes from a variety of sources, including position, status, expertise, and other factors. These are the people who can get things done (Kotter, 1995, Kindle location 79).

This group will become the "green berets" of your networked learning work—a highly skilled, elite cadre that will turn networked learning from a dream into a reality. Don't think of them as simply a handful of the most tech-savvy people in the school—far from it. Members of the team should come from a broad mix of stakeholder groups, including administrators, teachers, board members, support staff, students, parents, and community members. They will be the first to explore learning networks, argue about the educational implications, and wrestle with the change process. Later, they'll plan and guide your pilot program—leading meetings, fixing technology problems, celebrating successes, and making changes. Selecting the right team members is potentially the most important decision you can make to continue guiding your school down this path.

Building the Change Team

Depending on the size of your school, the change team will number anywhere from a few people to as many as twenty-five. Based on our experience, you will want them to meet at least twice a month, with small teams meeting for at least an hour and large teams for at least ninety minutes. In addition, members of the team should be expected to do two to five hours of work between meetings, such as reading materials, setting up their learning networks, and performing research. Keep in mind, their technology knowledge will typically range from expert to beginner.

Each member of the team needs to be a person who can make an impact, so you will want to look for team members with certain characteristics, most of which can be identified by answering the following questions:

- Does this person have a key role or responsibility that necessitates her presence on a project of this importance? Is she someone who plays an important role in the community or connects several different stakeholder groups? Does she have the power to get things done?

- Does this person possess natural leadership skills? Is he someone to whom others look for guidance even though he does not have a formal title?

- Does this person have advanced technology skills that would enable her to set up 21st century tools for the team, teach people how to use them, and support them when they have questions?

- Does this person already use networked learning environments in his daily work, or can he learn to do so quickly and be able to share his expertise with others?

- Does this person have an understanding of teaching and learning that would provide a helpful context for the kinds of ideas that will be discussed? Does she "get" kids and classrooms?

- Does this person have a positive attitude and a deep understanding of the stakeholders? Is he well liked and well respected in the school community?

If anyone has at least one of these qualities, put him or her on the list of potential team members. Don't hesitate to use these questions to solicit recommendations from colleagues, community members, and even students. This isn't about picking people who like the technology; it's about selecting a group that can bring about change. Here are some keys to remember when you start narrowing down the list:

- Everyone on the team should have an openness to change. It's probably the only non-negotiable characteristic.

- You will need some people in the room who have the power in their position to launch and guide schoolwide initiatives, get board approval, authorize spending, and so on.

- With so much riding on the technology for this project, be sure to have at least one member of the technology staff as a part of the team. It helps to have someone who knows how to use learning networks, too.

- Someone in the room needs to deeply understand curriculum and instruction in order to talk about the impact of learning networks on student achievement.

- Teachers need to be in the room to make this work real and applicable.

- Remember that if this team is to effectively lead the rest of the school through the process, it must represent as many voices in the current school community as possible.

After this initial process, you should have a solid mix of roles and expertise. We urge school leaders to invite people to join the team via face-to-face conversations, not a phone call or an email. In fact, we think it's a good idea to set aside fifteen minutes or so for each potential team member in order to offer that first draft of the compelling case, convey your own excitement, outline what their participation might require in terms of number of meetings and hours of work, and answer any questions. If they don't have a foundation in the ideas that you are discussing, you may even want to follow up with one of the following video links that we recommend. Don't downplay the level of commitment to the process, but don't scare them off, either. Remind them that any undertaking worth doing is going to take time and effort. As much as possible, make this an invitation to a long-term discussion around real, important change that will impact every student and teacher in your classrooms.

A quick word about students and the change team. We sincerely believe that students provide terrific insights and are an indispensable part of any change team, but we also recognize that some teams feel uncomfortable speaking frankly about challenging school issues when students are part of the conversation. So while we personally recommend that you have students on the team, it is a decision that each school will need to make individually.

If you decide to not have students on the team, another successful approach is to create a "student change team" that meets separately, goes through a similar process, and gives insights on topics discussed. Sometimes having a separate student team can be more effective than integrating students into the main team. A group of students talking with their peers will often speak more candidly about the changes they believe are needed than they would in a room filled with teachers, staff, and administrators. Either way, make sure you include their voices. We guarantee they will have indispensable insights that the adults will miss.

In the end, you want a team of excited, committed people who are willing to push themselves and each other in seeing the learning world in a different light. They may not understand the bigger picture at the outset, but they will feel like they are a part of a meaningful learning journey for themselves and for their school.

Starting the Work: Meeting 1

Your first meeting should be about building energy and excitement. It's a kick-off event that will solicit buy-in and set the tone for the work to come. Send team members an official email invite that includes a brief agenda and a link to a video to watch before the meeting (more on this in a moment). The meeting will have three parts: (1) you will share the compelling case with them, (2) you will lead them in a discussion of the short video you asked them to watch prior to the meeting, and (3) you will set the table for the next meeting by talking about the work of the team and assigning some "homework."

Start the meeting with a ten-minute talk about why you believe schoolwide adoption of learning networks is important—the compelling case. You will want to talk about how the world is changing as you see it, why networks are important to learning, and the implications for students in your classrooms. We suggest staying at the fifty-thousand-foot level and letting the team fill in the details that are most relevant for your school or system. If you create slides, avoid using a lot of text. Go for compelling photos and key words that will get people thinking about change. If you want inspiration, see Harvard professor Lawrence Lessig's style of presentations (Reynolds, 2005). Visit **go.solution-tree.com/technology** for more information on Lessig.

Next, provide opportunities for team members to talk, so that right from the start they understand they will have an active role in the process. To that end, we'd suggest framing a discussion around the video you asked them to watch prior to the meeting. The video will set the tone for the conversation and also give them something to talk about during the meeting. Here are three Ted Talks (www.ted.com) that we particularly like, but feel free to choose your own; each is less than twenty minutes:

- Sir Ken Robinson's "Bring on the Learning Revolution" www.ted .com/talks/sir_ken_robinson_bring_on_the_revolution.html

- Michael Wesch's "From Knowledgeable to Knowledge-Able" www .youtube.com/watch?v=LeaAHv4UTI8&feature=player_embedded#!

- Sugata Mitra's "The Child-Driven Education" www.ted.com/talks /lang/eng/sugata_mitra_the_child_driven_education.html

All three of these videos offer some compelling rethinking about education that should lead to some great conversations among the team. We like to ask team members three questions regarding the video (you can include these in the email): What do you agree with? What do you disagree with? What does this make you think about education in the 21st century? Typically, we ask them to pair up and share their answers for ten minutes or so, followed by ten to fifteen minutes of the whole group compiling a list on the board or projector. As these responses are shared, we urge facilitators to gently probe and ask follow-up questions to help draw out as many viewpoints as possible. The goal here is for everyone to share. Gather all of their answers, and dump them into your online space (more on this in a moment); these ideas should be added to your compelling case at some point in the future to make it stronger.

Finally, the remainder of the initial meeting should be spent talking about the steps for moving forward. At this point, talk about the three intertwined topics that will form the bulk of what this group will discuss: (1) learning networks, (2) the landscape of networked education, and (3) organizational change. Explain that you'll be starting with learning networks and that the emphasis will be on team members' *own personal practice* and how networks can apply to their own learning. At this point, we'd humbly suggest assigning as homework the first two chapters of this book and asking them to explore one tool mentioned in chapter 2. In addition, before you wrap up, find out what questions team members feel still need answering. What logistical issues need to be addressed in terms of meetings and communication? Let them know that the meetings are a work in progress and that you want their input and ideas to shape future work.

One final thought—you'll note we didn't use much technology in the first meeting. That's by design. If your team members are like most, they are walking into this first meeting feeling anxious about the technology. That's why we like the first meeting to focus on the ideas—why the world is changing, what learning networks are, and how they affect education. After your team gets its feet on the ground with these topics, they can start learning with the tools in the second meeting.

Learning in Networks: Meeting 2

The second meeting is about diving into the world of networked learning. Before discussing specifics, let's note that there are two things that should be in place for all remaining meetings. First, everyone should have access to a computer, so have members bring their laptops if they have them or, if not, pick a meeting place with access to computers. Second, have technical support available if possible, preferably in the room during the meeting. It can be frustrating to lose valuable meeting time because of a small technical glitch.

A good activity to begin the second meeting is to give everyone the opportunity to share in small groups their experience with reading chapter 2 and trying out one of the tools (the homework that you assigned at the end of the first meeting). Have participants discuss which tool they picked and what they learned. It could be a technical understanding, a realization about networks, an emotional hurdle, or an abject failure. Many will have had a tough time with it; sometimes sharing mutual struggles is the most fun and revealing part of this meeting. The important thing is for everyone to honestly reflect on the experience. Don't let anyone talk about changing your school at this point. That conversation will just bog things down at the beginning, especially if people do not have a strong enough understanding of learning networks and the shifts taking place in education in general. We like to announce at the beginning of this meeting that the work of the change team right now is to concentrate on their own learning and passions, as we talked about in chapter 2. If members feel like they want to bring up ideas for your school, create a "parking lot" in your online space, a place where people can store these ideas for later discussion. Then you'll pull things out of the parking lot when you get to the pilot stage.

Next, have someone who understands the tools fairly well lead the team through a hands-on activity where members create accounts and use them together. Choose one of the tools from chapter 2, and walk the team through the process of using it, giving everyone free time to practice. If you have time and your team is up to it, you can teach more than one. If technical help is available, have that person coach anyone who is further back on the learning curve. Don't worry about individual progress. The important thing is that everyone walks away with the ability to participate in a learning network before the next meeting.

At this point, we would also strongly suggest the introduction of a shared space online for team members. Ning (www.ning.com) offers an environment for educators to do just that, a closed (or open if you like) Facebook-type space where team members can carry on discussions, share photos or videos, write blogs, and more. For a great example of a school-change Ning site, check out the "St. Joseph Digital Express" (http://saint josephschools.ning.com/). Or, if you have your own learning management system, such as Moodle, you can set up shop there. (Note that this will require a bit of setup and practice on your part beforehand.) Save some time during this second meeting to help your team get acclimated to its online space, and outline the expectations for its use—to hold discussions, share resources, ask questions, and so on. As a first step for participation and a bit of "homework," ask your members to share their own hopes and fears about moving forward in a post to the site. At a minimum, dedicate an area of the site to technical support and encourage the team to post questions there. Ask your tech-savvy team members to regularly check in and answer them.

That second meeting is also a good time to create a "tag" that will help identify bookmarks, tweets, or blog posts that refer to the team's work, perhaps something like "hcchange11" (in this case, the "hc" represents Hunterdon Central, and 11 refers to 2011). At each meeting, you might quickly review the items that the team has tagged since the previous gathering. We suggest using whatever tools the team members have the most familiarity with or are willing to learn. The key here is not to overwhelm participants or get hung up on the technical aspects; do what's easiest, and be patient.

Picking Up Speed: Meetings 3–8

Note that in the first and second meetings the team focused mostly on spending some time learning about what networks are, how they facilitate learning, and what the tools are for making that happen. We find it's best to dedicate the next half-dozen meetings to learning more about the network and adding to the mix a rich discussion of how this global web of connections changes the field of education. Also remember to avoid discussion of how these will be used in your offices and classrooms! Put those questions in the parking lot, and wait to discuss them later. (By the way, we didn't pull *eight meetings* out of the air. If you are meeting every two weeks, eight meetings is four months, and our experience has shown that's about how long it takes for people to really wrap their brains around these tools in a networked learning sense. The time that you need to complete this work may vary a little, but three to six months is the norm for most teams.)

There are tons of materials to get you started, but here are a few that we have found useful. (Visit **go.solution-tree.com/technology** to access these and other links.)

"New Study Shows Time Spent Online Important for Teen Development" (MacArthur Foundation, 2008): This terrific study reveals that "youth are developing important social and technical skills online—often in ways adults do not understand or value." Among its findings are that "Young people are motivated to learn from their peers online."

"Fluid Learning" (Pesce, 2008): Mark Pesce explores the loss of control that we are experiencing as educators and makes recommendations to promote flexibility and fluidity in our classrooms.

"Minds on Fire: Open Education, the Long Tail, and Learning 2.0" (Brown & Adler, 2008). This seminal essay discusses the effects of networked social learning on traditional classroom structures, specifically in higher education.

The 2010 Horizon Report (Johnson et al., 2010): This report talks about the importance of social learning and gives examples of it in an online environment.

"From Knowledgeable to Knowledge-able: Learning in New Media Environments" (Wesch, 2009): If you enjoyed the Michael Wesch TED talk that we recommended previously, you will love this similar discussion of how the new media environment is disrupting current teaching methods and philosophies.

"Footprints in the Digital Age" (Richardson, 2008): OK, you knew we would sneak one of our works in here. This easy-to-read article talks about the shifts taking place with education, the new literacies children need to know, and how teachers can get them there.

"Learning: Peering Backward and Looking Forward in the Digital Era" (Weigel, James, & Gardner, 2009): This great article places the changes we are experiencing in a historical perspective.

"A World to Change" (Downes, 2010): Stephen Downes shares examples of online learning that will promote "a complete redesign of the system, from the ground up, using new technologies and new ideas."

Learning From the Extremes (Leadbeater & Wong, 2010): This Cisco-funded document discusses the international implications of many of the ideas we have discussed, specifically many of the structural challenges.

National Education Technology Plan 2010 (United States Department of Education, 2010a): This plan is a clear clarion call from the U.S. Department of Education to apply "the advanced technologies used in our daily personal and professional lives to our entire education system to improve student learning, accelerate and scale up the adoption of effective practices, and use data and information for continuous improvement." It is a terrific resource to use with boards of education and other stakeholders looking for government support of these ideas.

"How Is the Internet Changing the Way You Think?" (Brockman, 2010): One hundred seventy-two essayists reflect on how the Internet is changing their thinking.

Most importantly, you will want to select some activities to engage people in the learning process in ways that use their networks and motivate them to find resources like the ones just listed, as well as people to discuss them with. Here are some activities that schools have used to move their teams forward (from the easiest to the most challenging):

- Set up "buddy systems" within the team—pairs or trios of individuals who work together to explore one or more of the learning networks. They can share successes and failures at meetings, ask each other questions, and lend support to one another.

- Have unfamiliar team members try to learn more about each other by going online and searching for evidence of participation. Have them share what they learn about each other online. A fun exercise can be to determine who on the team has the biggest "online footprint."

- Use your networks to reach out to other educators who have started using learning networks in their schools, and ask them about their experiences, what they have learned, and how they have handled this transition. (There are several of these educators listed in this book, and you will find many more once you start to use the networks.) Have team members share the results of their research by showing the conversations within the network tool in which they took place—for instance, show the Twitter conversation, and talk about it.

- Have guest educators who have undergone this transformation participate in a meeting virtually through Skype to talk about their use of the tools in their work, their classroom, and so on.

- Have team members take a stab at rewriting the compelling case using the notes from the initial meeting and other exercises completed by the change team since the very first meeting.

- Assign members of the team to perform research in their area or discipline, such as finding out more about how learning networks can be used in history, science, school administration, and so on. Give examples at the meeting of what teachers and administrators are doing in these areas at other schools.

It will take some time for people to start understanding the truly powerful implications for education and to start thinking about how to encourage the use of these tools in your school. People will progress at different speeds, and everyone will not always agree. It is important to talk through difficulties with learning and differences of opinion at the table, even if that means putting an agenda item or two on hold. Think of this time as an investment in a solid foundation of everything your school will do in future years.

Your team can see this multipronged approach in the experience of John Carver, superintendent of schools in Van Meter, Iowa. His district is on an impressive trajectory toward infusing these networked learning interactions in its classrooms, but that wasn't always the case. John started by making the compelling case for change. "I started the ball rolling by sharing information with my team about the position of the U.S. economy in the world and the failure of schools to move forward," John said. "And I talked about these emerging technologies and the way they were changing learning in this century. From there I engaged my team in the process, both intellectually and emotionally, and I listened to what they had to say" (J. Carver, personal communication, September 3, 2010).

And engage he did. He had discussions with the building leadership team about change; had everyone read *Who Moved My Cheese*, a best-selling book about change; and had each person identify not only themselves in the book but also three of their friends. The leadership team then took turns presenting at staff meetings about how the field of education needed to change the way it did its work and how modern technologies changed the game both in and out of the classroom. They began using the tools, participating in Twitter networks, and building large and active networks. Finally, they discussed what each of them could do in their areas to make this a reality—the things that would get people excited, motivated, and move their understanding forward. Most importantly, they began regularly using the tools at school and at home.

You'll know your change team is ready for the next step in the process when participation in networks no longer seems scary or foreign. For some it may become a natural part of their day, but for most it will still be a struggle to remember to check their network. That's OK. Habits are hard to form, and you need to give people time. They are trying to learn in a whole new way. You just want to emerge from this process after your eighth meeting with a common understanding of networked learning and a shared understanding of how these tools might be used in the education space. At that point, you are ready to talk about using the tools in your school. You are ready to design your pilot.

Cornerstone 3: The Pilot

After eight meetings or so, when your team has immersed itself in the shift conversation, you'll want to start designing a plan to broaden the use of learning networks beyond your change team by engaging a large segment of your school in a voluntary pilot. Don't wait until everyone has a deep understanding or complete unanimity to start working on the pilot. In fact, it can actually be helpful to still have a couple of people struggling and some disparate points of view as a check that the pilot you develop will work for people who adopt the new changes more slowly. Understand, however, that before you can begin thinking long term, it's imperative that your change team is able to see the world differently on a practical, pedagogical, and systems level. The litmus test for whether your team is ready for a pilot is whether you (1) understand the power and importance of networks to student learning, (2) embrace the fact that the use of these networks may disrupt some of your traditional educational approaches, and (3) are ready to discuss the types of changes at your school that will support this work. That's because the pilot is a larger version of the transformation that your change team has undergone. It is an opportunity for lots of teachers (and potentially other stakeholders) to start participating in learning networks themselves and to talk about the impact on education and, eventually, their individual classrooms.

We suggest a pilot, as opposed to expanding the program immediately to the whole school, for at least three reasons. First, if you are going to use learning networks throughout the school, you're going to need a critical mass of people, as many as 10 to 20 percent of your staff, to provide the necessary support to ensure success. Schoolwide rollouts go more smoothly when there are dozens of "cheerleaders" who have already experienced success. Second, a pilot lets you work out the kinks by allowing you to test your professional development plan, technical systems, and other key components required for schoolwide adoption of learning networks. Nothing is worse than than rolling out the idea of PLNs to the entire school only to find that you don't have enough Internet access or that the meeting schedule isn't working. Third, a pilot lets you address questions of money and politics on a smaller scale. It is easier to get buy-in from stakeholders for a voluntary pilot than it is for a schoolwide rollout, and you will need less money to support the expenses of a pilot program compared to a full rollout. Finally, the pilot can give you the data you need to support a larger project.

We also encourage people to start small and build up, because we know it's actually the fastest way to spread adoption of these tools. This may seem counterintuitive at first, but it's true. If you teach a subset of your school how to learn in networks, their positive experience will spread throughout the rest of the community and quickly attract many more people in the process. On the other hand, if you attempt to teach more people than you have time to support, their negative experience will discourage others from participating, creating a domino effect that can adversely affect future work. In the end, the fastest way to engage all of your stakeholders in learning networks is the path that delivers the best experience and attracts many others to the program. The pilot won't be the end of your exploration—far from it!—but it will be the end of the three milestones we outlined for your first year, and it will take you pretty far down the path to using these tools throughout the community.

To design a pilot that works for your school, your change team should continue to meet according to the same schedule as before. In these meetings, your change team should discuss the answers to the following questions about the upcoming pilot program:

- Who will participate in the pilot, and how will they be selected?

- How long will the pilot run?

- What skills would we like participants to acquire?

- How can we create time for everyone to engage in the work?

- How can we ensure that people stay motivated and engaged?

- What partnerships could we create that would support this work?

- How can we ensure the necessary technology infrastructure and support?

- How can we ensure the right policies to promote networked learning?

You'll want to gather your answers to these questions in a short document, probably a half dozen to a dozen pages in length. (A Google Doc might be perfect for this.) This will become the plan for your pilot—a living, breathing document that you will discuss and adjust along the way. We will talk more about how to format the plan after we answer the list of questions.

So, with that, let's build a pilot, shall we?

Who Will Participate in the Pilot, and How Will They Be Selected?

First, the team will need to decide the number of pilot participants. A good size is between 10 and 20 percent of your school staff—less than that doesn't deliver enough of a critical mass to gather feedback and test your systems; more starts to get hard to manage. Obviously, in smaller schools, you may want to adjust those numbers up a bit. It's critical that participants come from every academic department in the school, and it's helpful if some of the nonacademic departments participate as well. You want this broad participation because in subsequent years as you expand the program, you want every department in the school to have someone with experience.

For selection, you can use the same criteria as you did for choosing the change team—official leaders, informal leaders, people curious about technology, people with a good understanding of teaching and learning, and so on. It's critical to involve department leaders, principals, and other supervisors in the process, making sure that some of them are part of the pilot and that all of them recommend teachers. In general, anything you can do to promote ownership of the project by all stakeholders is a good idea.

After you have begun to outline how many faculty will be involved, talk about other stakeholders. We find it helpful to involve some academic support staff such as librarians, counselors, special education personnel, and others since they often have terrific ideas about using learning networks in the classroom. We also like to hold meetings with parent groups during the pilot to educate them about the shifts, have conversations, and report progress. Perhaps even consider having a parent night where they can come and learn how to use the tools. You will also want to update the school board on your work and share the ways in which teachers and students are becoming connected. If you have a student on your team, you can have him organize a group of students to talk about learning with these tools, although that might be more appropriate later.

How Long Will the Pilot Run?

While a pilot can run for any period of time, we suggest you think in terms of one year. Remember that we previously suggested that the change team hold eight bimonthly meetings, a total of about four months? We did this because we find that this is how long it takes a group to really wrap their heads around networked learning. The reason we suggest one year for the pilot is because the participants will also need approximately four months to learn about the tools, and then you will want to give them time to practice what they have learned, share their experiences, and get feedback to improve. In the context of making the shift to networked learning at a school level, we think one year can get you pretty far down that road. As an added bonus, a full year of feedback and observation will give you a good amount of data that will influence your path going forward.

What Skills Would We Like Participants to Acquire?

As we discussed in chapter 2, the first part of this journey will be personal. When you are working with the pilot group, the focus at the outset should be on individual learning, just as it was with the change team. Remember, don't expect changes in classroom practice during the first part of the pilot, since teachers need to implement these tools in their own learning lives first if they are to apply them in their classrooms effectively. It will take months before teachers feel ready to begin using these tools and creating learning networks with their students. Similar to the change team, early on you should target the following learning goals for the pilot group:

- How networked learning differs from traditional learning and what the advantages are to learning in networks

- What the major tools for networked learning are, such as Facebook, Twitter, RSS feeds, social bookmarking, and so on

- How to log in to these sites, create an account, consume information, and contribute to the network

- How to regularly participate in these networks, including consuming and contributing

- How to create "online presence"; for instance, if you were to Google a participant, you would find his or her website, blog, Twitter feed, and other evidence that he or she participates in these conversations

- How to tap into learning networks for professional growth or school solutions instead of just brainstorming a local solution

- What impact learning networks have on education in general and, more specifically, on individual classrooms

When thinking about what you want people to learn, focus on the basics. Your aim is to get very high adoption of these networks, so quality here trumps quantity. Every member of the school community using one or two tools every day to participate in networks that excite them is better than a few of the teachers becoming superstars with their own blogs and the rest standing on the sidelines. Keep it simple, and continuously ask people to provide evidence of use.

How Can We Create Time for Everyone to Engage in the Work?

For the pilot, you are looking to create some extended time for the work followed by a series of meetings that allow reflection and follow up. If possible, we recommend starting the pilot with a "networked learning boot camp"—ideally a time early in the summer when participants can work together for two or three days to learn how to use the tools. This can be followed by meetings spaced evenly throughout the remainder of the summer or during the school year. Even though each school may take a unique path, we strongly advocate shared learning and practice time at regular intervals, even if it's just an hour of dedicated, focused time per month. Your pilot group needs to learn how to use the tools, reflect on how networked learning changes education, and talk about the changes in the school.

Schools have taken a myriad of approaches to creating this time. Some combine in-service days with after-school meetings that are also used for other purposes. Others set up cross-disciplinary learning groups with a member of the change team and organize them around common planning times. One district decided to inaugurate a series of early dismissals and late openings spread throughout the year so teachers could have dedicated time for discussion and practice. Others have offered summer professional development time when teachers could earn money by participating. And don't forget to take a long look at your current faculty meetings as well. We've seen schools take the time spent making announcements in faculty meetings and instead post them to a networked space online, allowing faculty to focus on their own learning during these times. It's good practice. In other words, schools need to be both creative and committed to finding ways to allow teachers to work both on their own and with each other.

When Lyn Hilt, principal of Brecknock Elementary School in Pennsylvania, wanted to engage teachers in a conversation about Web 2.0 technologies in the classroom, she knew she needed to find a way to make their learning a regular part of their work. "If you don't have an opportunity to learn about a new technology, practice it and reflect on it, it is difficult to use it effectively," Lyn says (L. Hilt, personal communication, November 10, 2010). So she began putting together a small group of teachers at her school and meeting with them regularly.

When she expanded the group to include teachers from three neighboring schools, a regular pattern of meetings emerged. Now, the teachers post new ideas to a wiki at the beginning of the month to start an online conversation about the tools. They get together face to face in the middle of the month to talk, brainstorm, and reflect. Then, at the end of the month, Lyn goes into the buildings to give them feedback and support on the use of technology in their classrooms. It's a continuous process of learning, testing, and reflection that supports good practice.

Your networks create time as well. We previously suggested that you set up a private Ning site for your change team, and this would be a good time to expand this internal network to the pilot. In addition to Ning, take a look at Yammer (www.yammer.com), a private enterprise social network that works particularly well for very large schools or districts. Platforms like Ning and Yammer allow all the participants in your pilot to talk to one another in a private space, an especially useful thing if you are running multiple pilots at different schools. While in general we recommend keeping your conversations public as much as possible, we believe that a private social network can be a very effective collaboration space.

How Can We Ensure That People Stay Motivated and Engaged?

Keeping people motivated is no small task, and it's harder when they need to learn new skills.

We believe the key is to emphasize that each individual carve his own learning journey at his own pace. It may be difficult for some people to hear that there is no single bar that everyone has to get over, but the really important subtext of this message is that you believe so much in each individual's ability to change that you will not require anyone to reach some arbitrary benchmark by a certain date. As author Alan Deutschman (2007) points out in his book *Change or Die*, people have a much higher success rate at changing behavior when they believe that others think they can change—a remarkably higher success rate, in fact. You can reinforce this with sharing successes at meetings or just by having a one-on-one conversation that recognizes someone's hard work.

In any educational innovation project, we are asking people to take risks, so your change team also needs to tell people that it's all right if they don't always succeed. We are asking teachers to walk away from established patterns of behavior and challenge themselves and their students to learn in different ways, and we guarantee you that the greatest fears of your pilot group will be the fear of doing something wrong. Teachers tell us all the time that they worry about the ramifications if using these networks does not go as well as planned. You and your team need to celebrate failures, rewarding the innovation and not worrying about the short-term results. Some superintendents start the first pilot group meeting by saying, "If you are not making some mistakes, then you're not trying hard enough." Some pilot groups read blog posts from teachers who have experienced spectacular failures in implementing networked learning but have laughed about it afterward and learned from the experience. However you do it, you need to create an atmosphere where trying new things is the norm, and the occasional failure is the price you pay for excellence.

After your teachers have some experience learning online, the most important source of sustenance for your pilot will quickly become the networks themselves. Participants will communicate with hundreds of their peers, and many will experience the joy of finding a like-minded community of educators who struggle with the same challenges and are looking for the same successes. It's a space to process failures, get feedback, and improve the results going forward. Your change team should use these spaces to recognize pilot participants' work. Principals can blog about the accomplishments of their teachers, and teachers can shout out what their colleagues are doing. Don't forget to recognize the students as well. Not only is this an opportunity to celebrate student learning, but the educators who work with those students will be motivated by seeing their kids recognized.

What Partnerships Could We Create That Would Support This Work?

One of the most unique and powerful parts of building learning networks is how they can be used to support any new learning, even learning about learning networks. Your pilot should include formal and informal interactions with educators at schools anywhere from across the street to the other side of the globe. For some groups, this may be a single interaction, while for others it might span the entire length of the pilot, but either way, it gives your pilot participants a real experience with learning in networks, and it models for them the work that they should initiate on their own.

Sometimes, rewarding participants' innovations can be about money, but not necessarily in the ways you would think. Schools rarely have the resources to do everything they want to do, but can you reward educators by spending money on the things they care about—on technology and tools for their classrooms? Eric Sheninger, principal of New Milford High School in New Jersey, has rewarded innovation in many of these ways. Eric rewards teachers who innovate with technology by making sure they have the tools they need to do the work, along with the necessary support and training. "Let them create a learning paradise in their rooms," he enthusiastically says. "If you are willing to reinvent yourself and learn new things, the least that I can do is give you what you need to do it" (E. Sheninger, personal communication, November 4, 2010). Eric also tweets the accomplishments of his team to thousands of followers around the world, letting people congratulate and cheer educators who are trying to make a difference with a new approach. He is sensitive to every small conversation as well, visiting classrooms to observe new projects for the first time. All of these approaches—some much cheaper than others—recognize hard work and celebrate people learning to live in a networked world.

We have seen dozens of examples of this in schools. Take, for example, Connected Principals (www.connectedprincipals.com), a virtual meeting place for school leaders from around the world. Through blog posts, Twitter feeds, shared documents, and more, this loosely organized network of learners provides information and inspiration to thousands of leaders and is one of the first places they go when they need support or advice. For another example, let's return to John Carver for a moment. He set up a partnership between Van Meter and a nearby school to advance their work on a complex curricular project. After creating learning teams at each school, teachers worked together online both asynchronously and in real time by trading documents, participating in chats, and getting to know each other. All of the secondary staff at both schools were involved, and the collaboration went a long way to not only fulfill the curricular objectives but also to teach skills about participating in personal learning networks. It was a brilliant combination of goals, set in a local context and scaffolded to meet the learning needs of those involved.

These partnerships work for a couple of reasons. Part of the equation is the act of making a public commitment, as Ian Ayres, author of *Carrots and Sticks*, says about motivation: "Other people matter. Mindfulness matters. And, participation matters" (Ayers, 2010b). An economist and professor in the Yale Law School, Ayres is quick to point out how public commitments are a terrific way to sustain changes that would otherwise be forgotten. We believe that commenting in public on a blog post, sharing a plan with a group of peers, or tweeting your ideas raises the level of commitment people have to this kind of learning. The other half of this equation is that these networks can also provide "expert advice," another element of successful change recommended by Alan Deutschman in *Change or Die* (2007). Your teachers, administrators, and staff need opportunities to learn from experts, try new skills, evaluate their success, and repeat the process over again. Having a network at your disposal often means starting with some outside help as well as having a just-in-time support group.

How Can We Ensure the Necessary Technology Infrastructure and Support?

Is your school's technology team ready to handle networked learning? Your change team needs to think about this question, and your pilot group needs to test their answers. We discuss all of this in more depth in chapter 5, and we suggest that your team read it before putting the finishing touches on the pilot plan. You need to ask questions about the number of computers at your school, the amount of Internet access, the school's acceptable use policies, Internet filters, and more. The answers will influence many factors of the pilot.

At a minimum, your pilot teachers need their own computers and Internet access. That's a non-negotiable. If your school is strapped for funds, we suggest using inexpensive netbook computers, which cost less than $200 (more on this in chapter 5). Wireless connectivity at school is great to have, since it provides a level of mobility that promotes use. Participants should also have Internet access at home. Most will, but for those who don't, you might want to work on that with them. If they have smartphones, they can be used during the pilot, too. Don't worry too much about the software at this point, since most of the programs will be available free through your browser. Also, we don't discuss budgeting for these items in this chapter, but see chapter 5 for more thoughts on the money side of this equation.

Another non-negotiable is support. Your technology personnel need to know that pilot participants will require more immediate support than the typical user. Having a member of your technology staff on the change team will help convey that message throughout the process. Hopefully, if that person has learned to operate in online networks with the rest of the team, he or she can also help establish and support your online space. Again, we talk a lot about support in chapter 5, so be sure to read that before making your final plan.

It's important that pilot participants are told to immediately report any technology hurdles they encounter so that your change team can work closely with your technology personnel to fix them. One of the main benefits of the pilot is to work out these issues in advance of a rollout to the whole school. If problems persist over time, confront the issues head on.

How Can We Ensure the Right Policies to Promote Networked Learning?

In schools in which networked learning is prevalent, teachers and staff members are, in a word, networked. They have personal (and perhaps professional) Facebook pages, Twitter feeds, blogs, and more, and the line between their work world and their personal world can begin to blur. Should a teacher write on her blog about the difficulty she is having achieving her goals in one of her classes this year? Is it all right if a principal puts a family photo on the school blog site as part of his or her holiday message? Should teachers "friend" students on Facebook? We discuss this in much more detail in the next chapter, but here is a primer.

We've seen each of these questions answered both ways depending on the district; obviously, there aren't any correct answers here, even in a legal sense. We know the easy answer is to just say no to everything, but that's not the best answer for the kids in your schools. These types of questions need to be answered collaboratively and clearly, and your change team may be a great asset in that pursuit. Have them explore scenarios, research what other schools are doing, and reach out to their own networks for ideas.

The results of these conversations can find their way into the staff responsible use policy. (We discuss this in more depth in chapter 5.) Like your students, every adult at the school should sign a document that clarifies his or her use of technology at the school. Like your student policy, administrators should look at the staff policy as an opportunity to encourage adults to make appropriate use of networks. Make it clear that social networks used for educational purposes are part of their role, and with that comes responsibility. Teachers can discuss their content and pedagogy but not give out student information. They can engage with other teachers and other schools, but they should work closely with school personnel if they want to set up networks for the school as a whole. There will be some trial and error here. The important thing is for the school to encourage access, even as it defines the limits.

From Launch to Wrap Up

Next you will want to announce the pilot to your school. We'd recommend doing this in a face-to-face meeting with all of your staff if at all possible. Get everyone together to hear the compelling case, followed by a brief discussion of the work of the change team and the proposed pilot. If you can't get everyone together in one place, send an email followed by a series of meetings led by you or change team members for various departments, divisions, or schools. Allow time for questions when possible, and remember that this might be the first time many people have heard of these tools, so they may feel threatened or defensive. It is important to maintain an open attitude during these meetings, similar to when you started your work with the team. Remember, you don't have all the answers, you just have a compelling story of why networked learning is important to educators and a proposed pilot for how your organization can start putting aside time and meeting in groups to learn more about using these tools. Emphasize to the skeptical that this is a pilot, and you want their help in figuring out the rest.

After crafting the pilot, your change team will support its implementation in countless ways. Some can run the selection process, serve as team leaders, or collect feedback from participants. Tech-savvy members of the team can help manage online spaces and teach participants how to use the tools. Team members can set up a principal's blog post, a district Twitter feed, or an internal learning network to model the shift.

Leaders that we've discussed in the book often take on this public role. Pam Moran, the superintendent we highlighted in chapter 1, maintains two blogs—one for the public at large and another for members of the immediate school community. In these spaces, she talks about topics as wide as the vision for the twenty-seven schools in her district and as narrow as the individual accomplishments of students and staff. Eric Sheninger's students call him Mr. Twitter because his tweets have gathered an audience in the thousands, and he uses his tweets to highlight work like we described in the pilot. Lyn Hilt is an active blogger as well, and she celebrates the accomplishments of her teachers and staff along the way.

No matter what the role, all team members should continue to meet regularly to review the progress of the pilot and make adjustments. Following are the kinds of things you will discuss in these meetings:

- What were people's reactions to the initial announcement of the pilot? What needs to be clarified? Should follow-up communications be scheduled?

- How is the selection process proceeding? Do you have more or less interest than anticipated? Can you make adjustments?

- What are participants' reactions to the initial meetings? Do we need to speed up or slow down the learning process? Are there new topics that we need to introduce?

- How is adoption going over time? Are people sticking with the learning even when it is difficult?

- Are there any success stories that your team has heard that can be shared with the whole community to sustain the momentum of the work?

- Are there any major technological hurdles that you have run into that need to be fixed as soon as possible?

- Have people thought of any new ways to support and extend this work that were not considered by the team in the original plan? Can you change things to allow this to move forward?

Your pilot will no doubt need adjustments along the way, some of which might be suggested by the participants. Don't be afraid of making these changes if you think they will improve adoption and learning. The key here is that the change team is actively involved in ensuring the long-term success of the project by monitoring progress, cheerleading achievements, removing roadblocks, and thinking of new paths toward success. Finally, as you did with the work of the change team, remember to keep careful notes throughout the pilot. You'll need them to make plans for the expansion the following year.

By following this outline, in one year you can go from ground zero to having your pilot up and running. It will be a terrific foundation for networked learning throughout your school. Congratulations!

The Pilot: A Case Study

At the beginning of this chapter, we highlighted Hunterdon Central Regional School District and the work of Lisa Brady, the superintendent. Hunterdon Central's commitment to networked learning is impressive, and its pilot is a terrific example of one way to answer the previous questions. We would like to outline the features of its pilot as a way to illustrate potential answers to the questions we discussed in the previous section. Full disclosure here—both of us were deeply involved in the design and execution of Central's pilot. This means we have firsthand knowledge of the process and the results, but it also means that the pilot will naturally reflect our thinking.

Central titled its pilot "Twenty-First Century Skills"; it entailed more than just networked learning. The pilot was made up of three intertwined themes—(1) learning how to use learning networks, (2) talking about 21st century skills, and (3) exploring one-to-one computing (a system where every student has his or her own computer; more on this in chapter 5). For the purposes of this case study, we are going to focus on the learning networks strand of the work, but visit **go.solution-tree.com/technology** for more about the other strands.

The team that designed the pilot decided to invite twenty teachers, about 10 percent of the staff, to participate. They designed a table that outlined the work for a year (table 4.1), accompanied by a detailed plan of about six pages. The application process, which took place in April, required potential participants to answer four questions, including what kind of impact they thought technologies could have on learning and how they would construct their ideal learning environment. The team received forty-six applications, and it was a difficult decision-making process. The group that was selected included teachers from every one of the eleven academic disciplines, one department supervisor, and two school librarians. They agreed to meet face-to-face seven times over the summer and once a month after school during the year.

The pilot began in June with a flurry of excitement as teachers met for two days to learn about personal learning networks and to talk about their impact on education. They participated in small-group exercises that taught them about the tools, and they used Skype to videoconference with leaders at other schools who had already begun to implement these changes. Each pilot participant left the two days with some homework, mainly to begin building his or her own personal learning network. Participants were specifically instructed not to think about the application of these ideas to the classroom.

As they met every ten days or so for the remainder of the summer, participants shared their victories and defeats. They all joined the Ning site that had been constructed for the team, many joined Twitter, a few took up social bookmarking, and some started blogging. At first, the going was tough. One teacher commented about writing her first blog comment, "Pushing the button on that mouse was one of the hardest things I have ever done. Knowing that my words would be out there forever, and I couldn't take them back, was so intimidating." Another educator shared a success story about finding teachers on the other side of the world who shared his passion for classical world history. His excitement was palpable as he said, "And they see me as an expert!"

By the end of the summer, most teachers had a good feel for the power of these networks, and all were thinking about how they could use these tools with their students in the classroom. They had long discussions about student safety and what students needed to know to use these tools appropriately in the classroom. Lisa Brady, the superintendent, met with the group to encourage them to take appropriate risks in their instructional design, knowing that not every idea would immediately succeed. "If we are

Table 4.1: Partial Sample of Hunterdon Central's Pilot Outline

Stakeholders	Spring Before the Pilot	Summer Pilot Work	Fall/Winter Pilot Work
Faculty	Announce project. Ask for pilot volunteers (target is 10 percent). Hold selection process. Announce participants. Develop training materials. Make partnership with another school.	Pilot team participates in seven days of paid professional development centered on the three goals, two days in a "boot camp," and then one meeting every ten days for five weeks.	Pilot team meets monthly after school. Pilot team presents their work at winter in-service.
Board	Present the project at the spring board meeting.	Give a more in-depth presentation to the board during one-day summer retreat.	Provide updates on the work at fall meeting. Invite board members to the winter in-service.
Parents	Include project in end-of-year letter.	Arrange presentations at fall parent meetings.	Present project at parent meeting. Present learning network work at parent/teacher conference night.

not making some mistakes along the way," she said, "then we are probably not doing our job."

Starting in the fall, all of the teachers introduced different tools into their classrooms. English classes blogged, Spanish students talked on Skype to native speakers from South America, English learners made short films and posted them on iTunes, math students co-constructed a wiki that contained a glossary of math terms for use in a one-to-one class in which every student used a computer every day, special education students put their work on the web for evaluation by outside readers, and on and on. The creativity that teachers displayed was literally boundless. But in addition to successes, there were failures. One class that eliminated its textbook in favor of online resources discovered that some students longed for the step-by-step structure they found in traditional textbooks, for example. A few students complained to their teachers that they wanted to learn "the old way," by receiving a textbook, a lecture, and a pencil-and-paper test. The teachers took Lisa at her word, pushing forward with new instructional strategies, and some bombed or took too much time. Stories were shared, and adjustments were made for the next lessons.

By the time the group reached midyear, they really hit their stride. Their work in the classroom began to deepen, and they were excited about the opportunity to refine their use of the tools in the second half of the school year. There was also a buzz at the school about the project, mostly positive, but to be honest, there were some negative feelings as well. For example, a few teachers not in the program needed to be reassured that their classes were just as important as those in the pilot and that no one thought less of their work. Overall, however, everyone from the board of education to the parents and the staff were intrigued and energized by the work done in these teachers' classrooms.

The success of the pilot laid the groundwork for a new team of teachers the following summer. When the pilot was announced in the spring, there was an even larger landslide of applications than the previous year. At the time of this writing, nearly half of the students and one-third of the teachers joined this program in just over a year, and the school was poised for a full rollout within three years.

Beyond the Pilot

So far, this chapter has focused on the first year—from the first stirrings of the compelling case, through the building of your change team, to the design and launch of your pilot program. We focus on this time because most schools will share common approaches and because it is critical to get the details right at the beginning of this process to ensure long-term success. After the first year, however, the path might diverge. Some schools will expand the pilot after only a few months, while others may wait until the following year. Some might make their expansion quite large, while others may think they have developed enough of a critical mass to involve the entire school. Whatever your path, here are a few thoughts to inform your post-pilot work.

First, think about time. What are the ways that you can use the success of the pilot to grow the amount of time dedicated to this initiative the following year? Can the pilot serve as a basis for increasing the number of in-service days? Can it be used to convert other meeting times into plans for the expansion? Also, think about time that wasn't available to the pilot group. For example, if the entire school is participating in the expansion, can you use department meetings or other times that were not available to your pilot group?

Next, think about leadership. We recommend using your pilot group as the leaders of subsequent initiatives. Have them recruit participants, teach classes, coach, mentor, or perform other roles. Have them share their successes at meetings so others can learn more. Have them share some of their less successful attempts as well, and let everyone see that you don't need to be tech savvy to get this—trial and error works. All of this will reward your first-year group for their hard work, and it will also reinforce their networked learning skills by having them teach others.

Ask yourself if you can look for other ways that will make networked learning a more integral part of the school culture. One of the best ways to build momentum is to hire networked learners to begin with. We know of many superintendents and principals who routinely Google job applicants, not so much to find a negative online presence but in search of evidence that they use networks to learn in their own lives. Do they host a blog for their local, state, or regional organization in their discipline? Are they commenting on trends in teaching and learning? Schools need to start looking for these skills and abilities in their teachers and staff before the first day of work.

After the first day of work, incorporate global learning networks into the systems that support and guide your teachers such as:

- Classroom observations

- Lesson plans

- Curricular design and review processes

- Instructional walkthroughs

- Accreditation processes

- Annual evaluations

- Mentoring programs

- Peer coaching

- Departmental supervision

- Professional development programs

Networks can be part of how these interactions take place, opening up possibilities such as mentors at other schools and peer coaching from around the world. This is particularly effective in departments with few members, or for teachers from a specialized discipline. Looking for evidence of networked learning in people's classes and professional development plans can also underscore the importance of the work.

Success Will Come

We end this chapter with an important point for everyone who undertakes this work. Success will take time and patience. By the time you reach the end of your pilot, you'll have a significant portion of the school learning in networks and changing their classrooms, but you will feel like there is a long way to go. It's all right. While speed is important, remember that the fastest schoolwide adoption will result from building a critical mass that will reach a tipping point and spread throughout the school. As you build on the work of the pilot, teachers will share tips with others in their department, students will start asking about using these tools in all their classes, and parents will ask about the program on visitation nights. Many will begin to ask for schoolwide adoption with the program. Stick to the plan, and expand your pilot at a rate that you can support. Be systemic.

The year that you spend making the compelling case, working with the change team, and launching the pilot will be an exciting and rewarding moment in your school. Remember to enjoy the learning.

CHAPTER 5

ENSURING SUCCESS OF LEARNING NETWORK ADOPTION

In chapter 4, we sketched a road map of how to lead your school in the adoption of learning networks. We described how to engage your personnel in the change process, and we gave you a guided path complete with resources that you could use to support the change process. In this chapter, we move beyond personnel and process to give you advice on four areas that you need to get right in order to ensure your success—(1) money, politics, and technology; (2) technical support; (3) school policies; and (4) resistance to change.

For that reason, when it comes to managing the change process, we're going to be less step-by-step in this chapter. More importantly, in this chapter, we'll try to give you the ideas you need to build systemic solutions and overcome the major points of resistance.

The big points break down like this:

- How can schools find the money to pay for the devices and infrastructure needed to support the use of learning networks?

- How can schools structure reliable and affordable technology and support to help students, teachers, and staff use the tools?

- What are the policies that schools need to implement in order to promote safe and effective use of these tools among students?

- How can schools overcome the inherent resistance to change that exists in every organization (answering the question "Yeah, but . . .")?

Every one of these issues has been overcome by schools at some point, and in this chapter, we'll show you how you can do it in your school. The truth is that ideas for saving money, improving support, changing policies, or shifting the culture can come from anywhere. For instance, we've seen the thoughtful creation of a lone networked classroom result in a domino effect that results in changing policies on social networking for an entire district. We've seen one teacher's inventive use of technology with his kids drive a school to launch student one-to-one computing pilots. In fact, if you are not in a formal leadership position, this chapter could be even more important to you since it gives you the arguments needed to convince leadership that all this is possible.

If you find value in the ideas that we've been articulating in this book, if you look at the world and see a different learning future for the kids in your classrooms, you can do this. Other schools have and are overcoming very difficult obstacles to change; so can you. It will take creativity, perseverance, and, as author Carol Dweck (2006) suggests, a "growth mindset" as opposed to a fixed mindset. But it can be done.

Hurdle 1: Money, Politics, and Technology

"OK, so how am I going to pay for it?"

It's the million-dollar question (sometimes literally) that we hear from educators around the world, and with good reason. In an environment where schools have a high percentage of fixed costs and very little discretionary spending, how can schools find the dollars needed to support the use of learning networks? Furthermore, the question of money is closely tied to finding political support for these programs. To answer this question, we first need to discuss what schools really need when it comes to academic technology. The answer is both less and more than you may think.

In reality, creating networked learning spaces for teachers and students actually requires less technology than you might think. The basics for networked learning are pretty straightforward: computers, a robust Internet connection supported by a school network, and some software that will manage your Internet traffic. That's it. Sure, in the classroom, wireless access lends mobility that is becoming more and more affordable, and an LCD projector can aid in collaboration and sharing, but those really aren't requirements to make networked learning work in your school.

But how many computers? Well, that's where the "more" comes in. We believe that to deliver the greatest benefit to student learning, every teacher and student should have his or her own device. For teachers, this is a non-negotiable, a reality acknowledged by almost every other white-collar profession, but if you buy into the picture we've been painting of the networked classroom, it's a necessity for most students in grades 3–12, too. Believe us when we say we know that last sentence might seem like an unrealistic fantasy for many schools; many educators think a computer for every kid is a vision for private schools or wealthy districts, and that it can't happen for their own schools. Even if they could afford it, they are convinced that their public would not necessarily support student one-to-one computing (or just *one-to-one* as it is called). We'll address that barrier a bit later, but from a money standpoint, let's look at some ways you can start to rethink paying for technology.

Saving Money With One-to-One Computing

A one-to-one environment can actually save you money. How? While it may seem counterintuitive, the key here is that *every* student would have a device. Think about it as a form of bulk buying, the same as you would do at a superstore, but benefiting you in many more ways than just the price on the product. Buying one device for each student and committing to using it in class and at home empowers your school to eliminate existing costs in other areas such as calculators, textbooks, student response systems, DVD players, photocopying, mailings, and more. If you also adopt often free, online applications to replace expensive software, one-to-one computing can not only pay for itself but can result in significant cost savings for the school. That formula of reallocating costs through one-to-one adoption is at the heart of our recommendations to you regarding budgeting for technology.

We will give a more specific example of some numbers in a little bit, but let's start by defining the environment you will want to create. There are four ideas at the core of this recommendation, four understandings that will underpin the philosophy by which you implement your technology. Basically, if you commit to living in an online world:

1. The only technology the school will need to buy is a computer for each student and each teacher.

2. Students and teachers will access everything online (in the "cloud"), supplemented by open source software.

3. The school will be paperless.

4. Families will access school information online.

This is actually "business as usual" for hundreds of schools across North America. Even the least expensive of today's computers are robust enough to replace a myriad of small electronic devices such as interactive response systems, graphing calculators, DVD players, and other pieces of equipment. The effectiveness of online software provides a stable platform for collaboration at a fraction of the cost of traditional software licensing. Paperless students and teachers using these tools and syncing information between multiple devices are actually more up to date, efficient, and effective, while saving the school money. Finally, operating in this environment is a great way to strengthen relationships with parents and other community members by providing more real-time information in an up-to-date way.

By making a commitment to the four ideas previously listed, here's what you can save in return.

- By buying a computer for each teacher and student, you save money by not having to purchase the following:

- All other types of computing and related items (desktops in labs, laptops carts, tablet carts, and so on)
- Handheld technologies (student response systems, MP3 devices)
- Legacy technologies (CD writers, calculators)

- By using the cloud, you save dollars formerly spent on:
  - Proprietary software such as email, file server systems, and so on
  - Expensive server hardware to host these programs
  - Portable storage (DVDs, CDs, memory sticks/flash drives, and so on)

- By going paperless, you save money by eliminating:
  - Classroom photocopying expenses (paper, toner, leases, repair costs, and so on)
  - Books (paper textbooks, paper novels, paper nonfiction books)
  - Printers (devices, paper, toner, and so on)

- By utilizing online access, you forgo the costs of:
  - School mailings (paper, postage, ink for printing)
  - Report cards and other assessments

How much money is this? Frankly, it is going to differ for every school, but table 5.1 is a sample from one school of its estimated savings per student, per year, by applying these commitments.

Table 5.1: Sample One-to-One Savings per Student

Computers not needed if every student and teacher has a device	$62.50
Ancillary devices not needed in one-to-one	$20.24
Servers and other equipment that can be replaced by cloud services (including electrical costs)	$16.53
Software not needed if using online apps	$31.25
Postage	$9.72
Printer and copy paper, report card forms, and so on	$32.50
Printing and copying ink and machines	$12.12
Replacement of some paper texts with e-textbooks	$24.62
Total Per Student Per Year	**$209.48**

That $200-per-student figure is a nice start, but it's actually more. Since each computer should last for three years, you'll actually have $600 to spend on each student if you planned a three-year implementation rollout. What's more, our findings seem conservative compared to some others. For example, Project RED's research identified thirteen areas for technology-based savings, which they estimate total $448 per student per year (Project RED, 2010).

Now, before we go through these commitments in more detail, we want to emphasize one important note. Getting to this kind of savings is a process. The implementation of these four core ideas is not going to happen overnight, and no school should institute a one-to-one computing program without laying the groundwork for it first. That foundation, which we outlined in chapter 4, includes teachers having their own computers and using personal learning networks in their own lives. If you don't create a foundation of knowledge and access in your teaching staff, your implementation of student one-to-one will not produce the kind of changes you intend. That said, let's take a look at each of these areas a bit more closely.

One-to-One Computing

What happens when the computers people carry with them include all of their electronic needs in a single device? Well, a lot, actually. You can eliminate costs for classroom desktops, laptop carts, and staff room and library computers, keeping only a few for video editing, CAD work, and other high-end applications. When everyone has an Internet-accessible device, a whole slew of other hardware and software becomes unnecessary as well. Think calculators, clickers, and cameras, for instance. That's because the web is now the home to a lot of the tools and functions that we used to have to download to our computer or add as peripherals. Look, for example, at eTutor's popular graphing calculator (www.e-tutor.com) or Poll Everywhere's free online response tool that can be used for formative assessment (www.polleverywhere.com). With built-in cameras and microphones and free editing software, netbooks are complete personal video and audio recording studios. Even expensive special education software such as graphic organizers, brainstorming applications, and text-to-speech programs are now replaceable with respectable free versions online. In most cases, we can do whatever we need to do more quickly and more cheaply on the web, and we get the added bonus of being able to share our work and collaborate with others much more easily.

Obviously, there is a slew of add-on devices that enhance the learning process, and we're not saying you shouldn't consider them. Flip cameras have become popular in the last few years, and we know that many schools and teachers love their projectors and interactive white boards, but we'd urge you to consider those tools only after *every student and teacher has a computer in hand*. It's the only way to make the transition to a truly networked learning environment at your school.

From a budgeting standpoint, the good news is that by 2015, a computer that students could use effectively for both classroom and personal use will cost about $200. Some companies have already begun selling smaller versions of netbook computers for around $100, about the same price as a good graphing calculator. So the first step to estimating the cost of such a program for your school is to multiply the number of students by $200. Add the expenses related to your school network and Internet connection, and you are starting to move toward a base cost for one-to-one computing. The cloud (which we discuss next) and the prospect of students using their personal devices at school could potentially make that number even smaller.

We would be remiss if we did not also remind you about E-Rate funding, also known as the Schools and Libraries Program of the Universal Service Fund, which is administered by the Universal Service Administrative Company under the direction of the Federal Communications Commission. Every public school in the United States, and each private school with an endowment of less than $50 million, is eligible to receive rebates from the U.S. government on the costs incurred for Internet and telephone access. If any students at the school are eligible for the federally funded free and reduced lunch program, the minimum amount that a school can receive through E-Rate is a 20 percent rebate of Internet and telephone costs. For schools with many students below the poverty line, those reimbursements can climb as high as 90 percent. Those reduced Internet costs blend nicely with the strategy of the "cloud."

Cloud Computing

More and more, the world is living in the cloud. This means that instead of installing programs on our machines and storing files on our hard drives, we're running our applications online and storing our files in repositories hosted by someone else. Probably the most popular example at this point is Google Docs, which includes a free word processor, spreadsheet, presentation tool, and more. Literally millions of people, and many schools, are using these tools as a regular part of their practice. While Google Docs may not offer all of the bells and whistles that Microsoft Office offers, the advantage is that everything we create with Google Docs is stored on a Google server behind a login and a password. That means we can access our documents from wherever we have an Internet connection, including our phones. In fact, we wrote this entire book on Google Docs—occasionally using a Google app on our smart phones. And it's not just Office-type stuff. We're talking photos edited with an online software like Picnik and then uploaded to a hosting site like Flickr, or videos edited and hosted at YouTube. We're even playing games against one another in the cloud these days.

Not to get too much on the Google bandwagon since there are other alternatives out there, but the "Google Apps for Education" suite also includes free accounts at Gmail, Google Calendar, Blogger, wikis using Google sites, video and photo hosting, and a lot more. It does have a proven track record; many large school districts have integrated Google's suite of tools into their daily business, and every public school in the state of Oregon now has access as well. Visit www.google.com/a/help/intl/en/edu for more information on Google Apps for Education. It's part of a much larger movement online to provide tools and resources to education free of charge, one that is also filled with opportunities for schools. Open source tools—programs created by teams of people and, in most cases, licensed to the public for no charge—are another example. Free, open source software that students or teachers can run on their machines includes OpenOffice—a suite that includes a word processor, spreadsheet, and so on—and Audacity, a program for creating podcasts and much more.

So imagine not having to pay any licensing fees for productivity software and getting free hosting for all of your (and your students') documents, email, and more. Think that might have some implications for your bottom line? We do. The economic benefits of the cloud go beyond just the cost of the software, however. Cloud computing means fewer "moving parts" to support as well. When you rely on Google for your word processing, you get their teams of thousands of engineers and the power of their multiple redundant servers all around the world. You get their automatic backups of your files. You also get their professional development, such as online tutorials that can be accessed by teachers and students not only during the school day but at home as well. This means your local support team can produce fewer instructional materials and respond to fewer support calls, allowing them to move from addressing software issues to dealing more with questions of teaching and learning (more on this later). This is something that is desperately needed since most school leaders acknowledge that they do not have enough money for technology support (Stansbury, 2008).

Perhaps the most powerful cost savings that could result from operating fully within the cloud is facilitating the use of students' own devices in school. In many schools, students have portable laptops that could function just as well as a school-provided computer, and the cost savings of letting them use those computers at school could be huge. By setting up a separate guest network for these devices, your one-to-one program could be a hybrid in which some students bring their own devices and others receive a device purchased by the school. If your school has committed to accessing applications and information online, then these computers can be Mac or PC, since all they need is an Internet browser.

In fact, student-owned devices do not need to be limited to a netbook or a laptop. Many schools that have moved toward the cloud are allowing students to use smartphones in school for academic purposes. The proliferation of iPhones and similar devices means that many students in your school may already have a wireless device and might be carrying their own Internet connection as well. What if you committed to letting students use those devices in the classroom to do their work? It would not only reduce your hardware cost, but in cases where students have an unlimited data plan, it would actually reduce the amount of bandwidth you need as well. As the Internet speed of these phones improve, there will be a day very soon where they function just as well as your computer does today.

There are a few concerns that educators raise at the idea of students bringing their own devices to school. The most prevalent worries are that students' machines might have games or other distractions that would not be installed on a school-owned computer. Some educators have also raised concerns about equity, such as will it be obvious to everyone which students can afford their own computer and which cannot? While we're not suggesting that letting students use their own computers doesn't pose some additional challenges, schools that have done it have found that these concerns can be mitigated through ongoing conversations with students and parents and with clearly delineated expectations for use. Also, it goes without saying that students are more apt to use computers well if they feel a part of a community of learning with technology. In other words, teachers and administrators should be modeling the fluent use of computers to learn with their students.

Paperless Classroom

The paperless classroom has been an elusive holy grail, much sought after and rarely achieved. First heralded in the 1970s and 1980s with the arrival of personal computing, the paperless idea has a long history of failure in business, at home, and at school. Even the rise of the Internet in the 1990s failed to stop the relentless piles of paper from accumulating in our classrooms and hallways. (Raise your hand if you printed out your emails.)

So why do we think that it is different now? Well, actually, there are many reasons. First of all, the rapid proliferation of cheap mobile devices with lengthy battery life and Internet access is a game changer that empowers individuals to access programs and documents anytime and anywhere. Netbooks have a battery life of eight or more hours, and smartphones and tablets can go even longer. In either case, the weight of the digital paper you can carry around in those devices is an attractive alternative to lugging analog paper copies. And then there is the access issue. Living in the cloud with mobile devices means never being without that important document or spreadsheet or presentation. If you need to, you can pull it up wherever you have access, or if you've planned ahead, you can download it for offline access as well. Furthermore, the cloud is also a gateway to online collaboration, which is far more convenient than working off of print documents. With Google Docs, for instance, a group of people from disparate parts of the world can be editing the same document in real time, watching each others' edits as they go. Physical paper is actually feeling more restrictive these days. The cloud means that for the first time, working without paper is actually superior in many ways to working with paper.

Second, digital content is exponentially more rich and varied than it was even five years ago. Take books, for example. Amazon sold more ebooks than hardcovers in 2010, and its Kindle application can run on any computer, Mac or PC. Many of the classic novels we use in schools are free in their electronic versions. (Free *The Adventures of Huckleberry Finn*, anyone?) Also, this shift to electronic media is building among textbook publishers, who are starting to make their content widely available in electronic formats. For an example of that on a wide scale, see the Florida digital textbook initiative (Mardis, Everhart, Smith, Newsum, & Baker, 2010) or many of the college programs (Young, 2010). The reality is that there is so much valuable free content online right now that we can create our own textbooks if we like. Lots of people are doing that already, in fact. Thankfully, we're printing less and less of that digitally created content and instead publishing it to the web, where it can be accessed more easily.

Third, the increasing quality of the applications available online means that it is much easier to organize your life and work online than it is on paper. For instance, Evernote (http://evernote.com) gives you the ability to easily capture text from documents and webpages, photos from your phone, audio from any number of devices, and more. The best part is that all of that content automatically syncs to a web server, which then sends copies to all of your other Evernote-enabled devices. So snip a couple paragraphs from a *New York Times* article while on your netbook, and within a minute or two, you can pull up that note on your phone or on any other Internet-connected computer you can find. Using something like Evernote in conjunction with a task management application like Nozbe (www.nozbe .com) means you not only have everything with you, but you also know the next thing you need to do on your task list at all times. This kind of organization is just not possible on paper, and all of our students and adults need to learn to work this way to be part of the modern workforce.

Fourth, environmental awareness is much higher than it has been at any other time. "Each year, Americans throw away enough office and writing paper to build a twelve-foot wall stretching from New York to California. (And that doesn't even include all the newspaper, magazines and catalogs we throw away)," according to the National Resource Defense Council's (NRDC) project on saving paper in schools (NRDC, n.d.). Going paperless is a commitment that saves money for the school while saving trees for the planet. It makes becoming paperless not only something smart to do, but something good to do. There are related health benefits as well; did you know that by the end of their teen years, close to 60 percent of youth experience at least one low-back-pain episode because of lugging around fifty-pound backpacks filled with paper (Arnsdorff & Carroll, 2009)?

Fifth, if we are asking our students to carry textbooks and print papers, we are not really preparing them to enter the digital environments in which they will work. Our teachers and students need to commit to trading information electronically—papers dropped in a teacher's online drop box with a time stamp to say when they were delivered, assessments returned electronically with comments typed in the margins, midclass check-in assessments done on student computers, and tests taken online when possible. These are the tools and techniques of the modern learner.

Finally, the savings are too large to ignore anymore. If you are not convinced by the reasons listed here, how does a 50 percent decrease in your copying budget sound? For some, that's a conservative estimate. Take a long look at your copier lease payments; per-copy fees; printer replacement expenses; paper, ink, and toner costs; and book budgets. It's a huge number. Hidden in that pile of paper alone could be your money for one-to-one computing.

Family Access to Information

In some schools, moving to the point at which all school information—be it report cards, announcements, or homework assignments—is shared only online will be a big challenge. But if you can get to that point, you'll be reaping more than just cost savings in terms of paper and postage. It becomes a way to engage your parent community in conversations about student learning.

Now, we know that a one-to-one program will give all families access to a computer, but not all will have access to the Internet. We've seen some creative strategies to get around this, however. Some schools have formed successful partnerships with telecommunication companies to offer Internet access to students at reduced rates. For example, at Hunterdon Central, the school administration negotiated a deal with a national telephone carrier to offer students on the federally funded free and reduced lunch program a satellite Internet connection. The telecommunications company provided free hardware to the students and also offered them free bandwidth, while the school chipped in with a monthly fee that was 50 percent less than the regular price. It is an excellent example of a way to give access to families that would otherwise be staring across the digital divide.

Another way to provide access to families is to let them know where they can find free local "hotspots" for access. Many local businesses such as cafes and bookstores now offer free wireless Internet in their stores, and many public places such as the local library have wired or wireless access for users. In some cities, there is a concerted effort to blanket the city in a wireless net, such as in Minneapolis (www.ci.minneapolis .mn.us/wirelessminneapolis). We've seen students produce a Google map of these places and make it available for access and updating to the entire school through the cloud. Some districts have also chosen to keep a library or other building open a little later in the afternoon or evening to allow students and parents to use their Internet connection, or they've worked with local businesses to create an evening location for students to do their work.

Once a majority of students and families have access, you can go paperless with them as well, providing student information online and folding them into the learning networks you have established. You can create a *portal* for your parents, a password-protected system that allows each of them to log in and access their son or daughter's classes, homework assignments, grades, and any other information that you want to make available. There are many free or inexpensive portal systems available, including open source systems such as Moodle (www.moodle.org), which is a particular favorite of thousands of schools around the world. During the transition to this system, make your paper documents available on an opt-in basis: people can sign up to receive paper communication, but the norm is electronic. You can also start modeling your own use of these online spaces. Why not deliver your annual, monthly, or weekly updates via blog post instead of parcel post, giving readers more real-time information and providing a mechanism for hearing their feedback as well. Having parents look at grades online on a regular basis, instead of waiting to be notified via mail a few times a year, is a great way to promote a constant conversation about student performance and to avoid the conflicts that can result when parents don't feel like the school has communicated student progress often enough. All of these solutions are better for student learning and better for the budget (Stock & Fisman, 2010).

Politics: Buy-In For Technology From Your Stakeholders

From a money and learning standpoint, we think these four core concepts will go a long way toward changing the culture of your school around technology and making networked learning possible for every adult and child you serve. Finding the money for technology is one hurdle, but convincing your stakeholders that the money is well spent is another. If we had a dollar for every time someone said, "We didn't have any technology when we were in school, and we turned out OK," we would be very rich indeed. How can we convince even the most skeptical of community members questioning the school budget at a public meeting that changing our practice and putting the cost savings toward technology is in the best interest of our students?

First, share with them the compelling case that you developed in chapter 4. This is your "elevator pitch," the essential reasons that students need technology in schools today. It's the conversation about the changing needs of learners in the 21st century, the power of learning networks, and how the tools promote and support modern learning. Next, if you have not already read it, take a look at Tony Wagner's (2010) book *The Global Achievement Gap*, in which he talks about the importance of 21st century skills in the modern workforce. It provides some very concise language that you can use when you communicate with stakeholders, such as the seven survival skills: (1) problem solving and critical thinking, (2) collaboration across networks and leading by influence, (3) agility and adaptability, (4) initiative and entrepreneurship, (5) effective written and oral communication,

(6) accessing and analyzing information, and (7) curiosity and imagination. Use demonstrations and concrete examples whenever possible, at first from other schools and, later, from your own classrooms. Remember, every interaction with parents or community members is an opportunity to emphasize that the world in which they grew up is not the world their kids are entering. We talk more about parent communication at the end of this chapter in the "Resistance to Change" section (page 133).

We know full well, however, that at the end of the day, you'll need to make the case about money as well. It can be made. Make sure you have on hand the cost savings that you project by moving down the path toward a digital learning environment. Talk often about the elimination of expenses for peripherals, photocopying, printing, software, textbooks, and the myriad of other savings you have accrued. Draw up a one-page comparison similar to the one we presented earlier in this chapter—on the left is the cost of one-to-one, and on the right is all the costs eliminated by it. Even if you have not yet reached the break-even point, you need to show that, in the long run, the technological solution is less expensive than current business as usual, and that from a learning standpoint, it's a necessary direction to take.

From a global-impact standpoint, emphasize how this plan will reduce the school's environmental footprint. If possible, estimate the weight of the textbooks, papers, worksheets, report cards, and mailings you are going to eliminate by using well-established metrics; for instance, one ton (907 kilograms) of recycled paper spares seventeen trees. It's one thing to tell the community that you are "going green"; it's another to tell them that you are going to eliminate two million dollars in expenses and save a thousand trees. These kinds of examples will make the initiative more appealing for those who care about the impact on the environment. We also urge you to get your students involved in these calculations and representations; this kind of shift produces all sorts of learning opportunities.

For parents of special education students, the arguments for electronic resources are deep and powerful. Many assistive technologies are available for free to students who have a computer, and the effects in the classroom are significant for student learning, including those that help visually and auditory impaired kids. Visit **go.solution-tree.com/technology** for a terrific list of these resources. We talked about many of these technologies previously, but we believe that the most effective way to display this information is a side-by-side comparison of the resources available to a student on paper compared to those available on a computer.

When you integrate all of these together, you can make the case that our students need to be involved in these networks for 21st century learning, and in the process, it will save the school money, reduce our environmental footprint, be healthier for our kids, and better meet the needs of every learner. That touches a lot of your constituencies and builds support for your programs.

Hurdle 2: Technical Support

The second hurdle you'll have to overcome deals with providing adequate technical support for teachers and students to move into these networked spaces. It's one thing to help your teachers and staff see the need for change and create a road map for doing it, but if the tools don't work like they're supposed to, very few people will commit to making the shift. Poor technology support will bring your learning network implementation to its knees. Your shiny vision and terrific plans will just gather dust (Martinez, 2010).

To avoid this disaster, you must build an effective support structure using a multipronged approach. Start by making sure that you reduce the scope of your support needs as much as possible. Next, you need to have the right kind of technology personnel. Finally, think about the role of students in supporting the work as well. Those first three steps can go a long way toward building a structure that will meet the needs of your school and make using technology something people will look forward to rather than dread.

Reducing the Scope of Your Internal Support Needs

From a hardware standpoint, when you commit to a single device for learning among students and teachers, you also commit to fewer moving parts, and in turn, fewer things that can go wrong. Supporting a single brand and style of computer is a lot easier than supporting a myriad of desktops, laptops, PDAs, and so on. If students are using their own devices, you're simply supporting their connection to the network, nothing else. In addition, cloud computing means less on-site server support. You get the idea: the simpler, the better.

In terms of supporting people's use of the technology, we need to teach our students and teachers to answer many of their own tech support questions by providing them access to online resources. That means we create a series of support videos using a screencasting software like Jing (www .techsmith.com/jing) that cover as much of the how-to functions (such as "how to create a new presentation on Google Docs") as possible. And your tech staff doesn't have to be the group that creates all of these resources. It's a great opportunity for teachers and students to share their own knowledge with the school community and beyond while simultaneously reducing the need for face-to-face instruction around fairly straightforward tasks.

Post your how-to videos and links to others online on a support page in the private school network that we encouraged you to build in chapter 4. These internal networks have become a mainstay in organizations across the world as diverse as Best Buy, Intel, Deloitte, and the CIA (Bingham & Conner, 2010). Having teachers participate in these internal networks not only reinforces their skills but expands your support team to include all of the other teachers, staff, and students on the network. There is no reason that the technology department needs to bottleneck answers to easy questions that others would be happy to answer.

Everyone needs to get comfortable using external networks as well. That's how Edmonton principal George Courous was able to get a new blogging platform for his school. George wanted each of the hundreds of teachers and students in his three Canadian schools to have a blog, but he was frustrated by the technical details that kept stopping the process. In search of an answer, George had run through the most likely Google searches and had read the online documentation. Instead of giving up or calling technical support, he asked for help on Twitter, tweeting out a description of the problem. The same day, a follower responded that he would be happy to help, and he not only taught George what to do, he actually configured the system for him.

Just by redefining how you use the technology and teaching your personnel how to search for help effectively, you can go a long way toward lowering the internal support load and redirecting your current support resources toward more important tasks.

Hiring the Right Personnel

No matter how good your users are at finding their own answers, you're still going to need skilled technology personnel to help along the way. We all know that computers break, Internet connections fail, and settings get changed on a regular basis. Also, since we are advocating one-to-one computing, there are going to be computers to configure, a network to maintain, and many other technical demands. As students begin to take these devices home and as your teachers learn to use new tools, the number of questions they have will grow exponentially. How do you find the money and the personnel to fix things quickly and efficiently when they do?

The key to answering that question is the philosophy that underpins the hiring and evaluation of your support personnel, and here it is: *every technology person delivering solutions to teachers, staff, students, and families must see the world through an educational lens of networked learning.* This means that they look for simple, reliable, inexpensive, and scalable solutions that will meet the needs of the users efficiently and effectively. They look to open up access to the web whenever possible, and they make it easier, not more difficult, for teachers and students to access the information they need. Depending on their role, they may be very technical people who have come to this view of the world through working in schools, or they may be educators who have learned the technical skills after spending time in the classroom. Either way, their first priority must be to create an environment that facilitates teaching and learning through networks.

This is a different philosophy than the one that informed the hiring of technology personnel in the 1990s and, to a large extent, in the 2000s.

During that time, technology personnel were hired for their technical expertise first. While technical know-how is still very important, your technology personnel should also know a lot about learning. A lot. In fact, your technology staff should be the most connected learners in your organization. They need to model the kind of lifelong learning in networks that we want our students and teachers to adopt, and they must be effective at teaching others how to do this too. If existing staff don't fit this mold, it's important to include them in your networked learning professional development. You might think about a day-long retreat where your technology staff can talk with your change team about the compelling case for the use of learning networks in schools and the long-range plan that informs the work. You should also talk to them about the four ideas in this chapter, especially about one-to-one computing and cloud computing. When possible, ask the technology team to brainstorm about the way the current systems support the school's future goals (such as your pilot) and which systems would have to change to align more closely with those objectives.

Amazing transformations in understanding take place when technology personnel sit side by side with faculty and administrators in the pilot. Often this experience gives them first-hand knowledge of the most common challenges their users face, and they become energized by fixing issues that matter. It's a good idea to extend these visits into the classroom as well, having technology personnel sit in on classes and debrief with teachers afterward about the technologies they used (or could have used) in their lessons. Tech personnel's understanding of networks will inform the effectiveness of your support process.

Student Roles

You'll need people who are open to student help as well. A huge untapped support resource in our schools is our students, many of whom are the most knowledgeable technology users in the organization. We have talked about how students can play a role on the change team and contribute to the pilot, but in many places, students are just itching to help the technology department get things done . . . in a good way. While we've all heard stories of students hacking into networks and getting around filters, the vast majority of our kids want to help, not hinder, our efforts to integrate technology. Even in some of the younger grades, students can play the role of a hardware troubleshooter and software tutor. At lunch and after school, they can deliver equipment to classrooms and help teachers prepare technology in upcoming lessons. They can design online resource sites for teachers and students to learn more about how to use the technology, and they can run after-school sessions for other students. One high school went as far as to plan to have students run an evening help desk via chat. The potential and possibilities are many. Check out the *Generation Yes* blog for ideas and inspiration (http://blog.genyes.org/).

Your existing technical staff may see students as a threat at first. Many will bristle at the idea of a student doing "their job," and they may not like the idea of giving students responsibility for expensive equipment, but the fact is that the job might be impossible otherwise. According to Forrester Research, "large corporations typically employ one support person for every 50 PCs, at a cost of $1,420 per computer, per year. According to this model, a school district with 1,000 PCs would need a staff of 20 and an annual tech-support budget of $1.4 million" (Stansbury, 2008). As we know, most schools with a thousand PCs don't have anywhere near that number of support staff or budget. If you're going to move toward one-to-one computing, be honest with your technology team that students are essential. They not only have an opportunity to learn valuable skills along the way, but they also free up your technical people to perform other functions.

Hurdle 3: School Policies

One of the greatest frustrations for educators trying to embrace networked learning is that many of these tools and sites are blocked by their school, district, or state. Those who can access them often find rules and regulations in place that either explicitly or implicitly discourage use. This can include policies about a teacher's "online presence," student's at-home use of the tools, or others. In general, we've found that the default setting for online networks in schools is "off," something that obviously has to change if we are to expand a vision for networked learning for our teachers and students.

Educational organizations that are committed to the use of learning networks in teaching and learning should ask the following three questions:

1. Does our school block websites and programs that could potentially be used in the classroom by teachers and students to advance teaching and learning?

2. What is the school's policy regarding responsible use of learning networks by students?

3. Does the institution encourage use and provide for teaching students about them?

Blocking and Filtering

Almost all schools use mechanisms for blocking Internet content, especially in the case of younger children. Most schools in the United States follow the guidelines of the Children's Internet Protection Act (CIPA) since it's a requirement for receiving E-Rate funding. CIPA orders schools to block "pictures that are: (a) obscene, (b) child pornography, or (c) harmful to minors" (Federal Communications Commission, 2009). Beyond that, schools often block sites that use a huge amount of Internet bandwidth, such as gaming and video sites and specialized sites considered dangerous, such as sites that students could use to get around Internet filters. Still other schools block sites based on the request of individuals in the district. In the end, a school can block any site that it chooses.

We recommend a philosophy that balances safety with access, placing an emphasis on student education. While there is much on the web that obviously should be and, in some cases, has to be blocked, we suggest you take a long look at the social networking sites that students are using every day and ask yourself if you can teach them how to use these sites responsibly. YouTube is a good example. Yes, there are some objectionable videos on YouTube, but there are millions of opportunities to learn as well. Can you teach your teachers to teach your students to use the web well despite all of the "problem" parts? This emphasis on teaching students to evaluate and sift through content will be invaluable for them in all of their networked learning pursuits.

Whatever path you choose, be sure that the decision is a conscious one. All too often, these decisions fall to technology personnel or hired services with whom teachers have not communicated very well regarding what sites they need for their classes. Often, the people configuring the filters are given very little guidance. In the absence of any guiding philosophy, they are likely to be motivated by only one fact—avoiding the problems of blocking too little. Let's face it, a person might get some flak for blocking a site that a teacher needs, but he will most likely get fired if a young student is exposed to highly inappropriate material that could have been filtered. In short, the philosophy is block as much as possible.

To start an important conversation about what is and isn't getting through the filter, consider these questions:

- Who makes the decision on what you block? Are instructional personnel in dialogue with the technology personnel about the system?

- Why do you block what you block? Have you asked teachers and administrators what they need to use in class and out?

- Do you have different policies for children of different ages? How do you account for the needs of older students to learn to use the tools required in college and in the workforce?

- Do you block a site based on a single piece of objectionable material or because of the overall content of the site?

- Do you have conversations with students about their responsible use of these sites?

At the end of the day, networked learning requires access. We feel strongly that while there are dangers on the web, and while some content may not be suitable for students, we need to make that a curriculum conversation and not a filtering one. How do we educate students to make good decisions about their time on the web in schools so they make good decisions when they're not under our supervision? No question, this will require discussions and communication with parents and other constituents. Your stakeholders need to know that no system is perfect, and educating their child will not be an error-free process. It is impossible to create a safe haven in which no student or teacher ever sees a piece of content that they don't want to see, but we need to be willing to fight for the access our students need, not take it away.

Responsible Use

We're pretty sure that your current acceptable use policy will need a revision if you're serious about going down the networked learning path. While many schools have up-to-date, all-encompassing policies in hand, few have really geared them toward students and teachers making connections with others outside the classroom. In general, we've found the spirit of these policies to be focused too much on the "don'ts" rather than on the "dos." If we are to encourage our school communities to embrace technology and make it a part of their daily learning lives, we need to be focusing our expectations on the possibilities, not the pitfalls.

To start with, we prefer the term *responsible* better than *acceptable*. Both teachers and students need to be responsible for their use these days, not just behave acceptably online. Responsible use is something people will have to get used to; some standard practices by kids outside of school are hard to deem responsible. In other words, expectations will be high, but the expectation will also be that we are active participants who are learning with others, not just clicking on links and consuming information.

So think about starting with the "dos":

- Do use the network to connect to other students and adults who share your passions and with whom you can learn.

- Do use the network to help your teachers find experts and other teachers from around the world.

- Do use the network to publish your best work in text and multimedia for a global audience.

- Do use the network to explore your own creativity and passions, to ask questions, and to seek answers from other teachers online.

- Do use the network to download resources that you can use to remix and republish your own learning online.

● Do use the network to collaborate with others to change the world in meaningful, positive ways.

Obviously, some of those suggested responsible uses will challenge some of the traditional thinking that's gone into your current acceptable use policy. We're not suggesting that you adopt those ideas or any others you (or your network) may come up with without first believing they really are examples of responsible use. You have to own these uses first.

In addition, that doesn't mean the policy shouldn't spell out what irresponsible use looks like and what the consequences of it are. It should. You need to address cyberbullying, hacking, personal use, and more. Visit **go.solution-tree.com/technology** for examples of some great responsible use policies. But again, many of these types of problems are curricular issues, not simply use issues, and we don't think that should be the emphasis of the policy. We need balance—policies that discourage and address inappropriate behavior while encouraging participation in networks that support teaching and learning. Having discussions about social networking policies is a great way to engage stakeholders such as teachers, parents, and students in conversations about how to act appropriately and stay safe online.

Hurdle 4: Resistance to Change—The "Yeah, Buts . . ."

No matter how you go about it, no matter how well you plan, how compelling your case is, or how painstakingly slow you move ahead, you'll always have detractors and naysayers who will voice their concerns. Most will be polite, some may be less so, but along the way, you'll hear a number of what we call "yeah, buts"—all the reasons why, despite being an important shift to make for kids, it just can't happen at your school, at this moment. As long-time educators ourselves, we know most of these "yeah, buts" are valid realities to life in schools and that they do pose difficult challenges. But we also know that all of them can be overcome if we really believe in the mission to change what we do in the classroom and if we're willing to be a little flexible and a little creative.

First, we want to acknowledge that you are not going to win over everybody, and you shouldn't try. There will be a handful of people at every school, probably between 5 and 10 percent, who will dig in their heels and refuse to get on board no matter what. Don't waste time engaging with them. Instead, put your energy into supporting and spotlighting those who embrace the change. The face of your school should be the teachers who are looking toward the future.

Even among the willing, however, there will be some pushback. Once you commit to providing a laptop and access for every student and teacher in your school or district, you eliminate some of the biggest "yeah, buts" right off the bat, as in "we don't have enough technology" and "many of our students don't have access." But you invite many others. We're going to assume you've done a good job of making the compelling case for change to your staff, that you have conducted a pilot, and that you are providing a professional development structure for the remainder of the staff. No doubt, those are requirements to integrating any of these shifts in meaningful ways. Once those steps are complete, here are the most common "yeah, buts" and how to address them.

"I Don't Have Enough Time"

If there is one single reason that comes up more than any other from educators, it is the argument that there are not enough hours in the day or days in the week (or minutes in the hour!) to do this work. The busy lives of educators are a reality that we need to own. We know it's difficult to find the time for professional learning no matter what the topic, and it's particularly challenging when that learning is in a totally new arena that may be outside the comfort zone of teachers and students. But the reality is, we make time for what we value, and once we begin to understand how networked learning impacts our lives and the lives of our kids, we will find the time.

Here's the thing about learning in networks that may not be immediately apparent: it's actually a time *saver* in the long run. Eric Sheninger, a principal at New Milford High School in New Jersey, says that the power of the connections is in the ongoing resources and learning support they provide.

"People think that this takes more time, but it actually saves time to use social media since you can get answers to your questions very quickly," Eric says. "For example, I Tweeted out that I was looking to develop a new walkthrough procedure at my school and within minutes I had links to resources, pdf files of walkthrough formats and advice on what works and what doesn't. It would have taken me hours to search for this stuff, and even longer to write it all from scratch" (E. Sheninger, personal communication, November 4, 2010).

While there may be some more initial planning time to shift curriculum and personal practice as we learn how to use some of the tools and technologies, most teachers we talk with are amazed at how much easier it is to find and implement new ideas, communicate with colleagues and parents, and get their kids engaged in the work. The good news is that we're not talking hours a day of commitment at the outset. We usually advise people to begin with just fifteen to thirty minutes a day to build and sustain these networks. To some, that seems impossible. But hundreds of thousands of educators have made the shift; they've found a way to do it. Every one of them has sacrificed something in the process, but they've also found enough value in the end to continue learning and growing.

"It's Too Overwhelming"

For some, being plugged into these networks can feel like being thrown into the deep end of an icy pool. Just as you look at twelve items in Twitter, another hundred come rolling in. Before you know it, you've got a few hundred items waiting to be clicked in your RSS reader. There are blog posts to write, comments to leave, and bookmarks to check out. There's no way to get all of it done. This is a little different than just a lack of time as we discussed above. For some, it's a big shift to this idea of learning on the web, one that is much more random, distributed, and disjointed. Author John Seely Brown describes it as moving from "stocks of information to flows of knowledge" (Hagel, Brown, & Davison 2009). It doesn't make one type of learning better than the other, but learning in networks requires powerful new skills that we need to master in addition to the types of learning that we already know.

Remember that your participation will naturally ebb and flow in and out of these networks over time. Even the most dedicated bloggers will have a week where they don't post, and even the most avid reader will miss a week and have to skip a few thousand Twitter messages. As we mentioned before, we need to walk away from the idea of "doing it all" and learn what we can, when we can.

That's one of the most important take-aways to remind educators who are voicing this complaint. The environment they are struggling to manage is the same one students are going to experience each day when they go to work in their adult lives. Students will need to participate in these learning networks to stay on top of their fields of interest and to advance in their careers. If we don't teach them how to navigate these messy environments in our schools, if we instead teach them to learn from a book in chapters and to expect an "end," then they will be ill equipped to participate in the most powerful learning available to them during their lifetimes.

"I Have to Make Sure Kids Pass the Test, Get Into College, and So On"

Many educators will struggle to see how they can make sure students achieve all of those traditional outcomes while also making sure they have these new network-building skills and literacies. The simple truth is that until they do take on some of these shifts in their own learning, they'll struggle with finding that path to both. But it can be done.

As much as possible, it's important to celebrate the successes of teachers who do manage to integrate these new learning environments and whose students are successful by current standards. Ask these early adopters to present to the staff either in person or online, sharing their strategies and showing how they align new tools to old expectations.

"I Never Learned This Way"

This one is from the parents. While more and more parents are starting to understand the potentials of social networking sites like Facebook, many still need to be convinced that putting their children into networked learning spaces is a good idea. As part of your change process, you need to communicate with parents as much as, or more than, you communicate with the teachers and staff members within the school. We already suggested having parents on your change team, but you will need to find ways to reach out to the rest of parents on this issue.

Start by sharing the compelling case with them. Do this at regularly scheduled meetings with parent associations, as part of your parent mailings, emails, and on days that parents visit teachers. Lisa Brady from Hunterdon Central took this a step further and recorded a short video that essentially laid out the compelling case and talked about upcoming changes in the classroom. This video was shown in classrooms during evenings when several thousand parents visited with teachers to review their children's progress. Consider sharing the work of specific classes as well. Highlight on your school website, or better yet on your blog, students and teachers using these tools to learn in more effective ways. The more concrete examples you use, the more successful your message will be. That's because discussions about learning networks without examples will most likely be misunderstood by a parent who has never participated in one.

Also consider having students offer evening classes for parents in learning networks. Many parents, especially those with younger children, want to know more about sites like Facebook. You might try a Facebook Night at the school run by students who have worked with a teacher to create a plan for showing parents how to use the tools. It's a great way for students to demonstrate how much they know and take on a leadership role while providing a bridge that will help parents understand what is going on in your classrooms.

Finally, invite parents into your networks. Several of the principals we highlighted have numerous parents as Twitter followers, and it is one of the easiest ways for them to instantly share good news with a subset of the community. Some schools allow parents to post comments on stories and blog posts on the school website. (We know, it sounds scary, but it actually works pretty well.)

The more you can do to educate your parents about learning networks and to make successes in the classroom transparent to the larger community, the more they will embrace and support their use in the classroom.

"I Don't Want to Make My Life or My Work Public on the Web"

We understand that this is a real concern for many adults who are beginning to make the move to the web. The move from private to public is a difficult one, especially in a culture of education that has been functioning primarily behind closed doors for the last one hundred years. Depending on how you look at it, it's the unfortunate (or fortunate) circumstance of teaching at a moment of huge change. While the compelling case may sway some to begin being more transparent, for most it will take more convincing.

Once again, modeling transparency is the key. Leaders need to be sharing their ideas and connecting with others, showing their "network literacy" whenever they can. And teachers who are making these shifts to a more public presence should be highlighted as well. We've seen districts that have created special web pages to promote the work of educators and provide links to their personal blogs as well. Any kind of promotion on the part of the school can demonstrate to people that participating in networks is a professional expectation.

Finally, we need to build school cultures that are focused on sharing and participating widely within these learning networks. The greatness of the web is that at its core, it's a vehicle to share our ideas and help the world become smarter. By putting our lesson plans online, there's a chance that teachers and students half a world away can share in the learning. That participatory stance is crucial for everyone in the school community to understand and model whenever possible. In other words, sharing publicly should simply be another piece of our schools' standard operating procedure.

"I'm Scared"

Sensational news stories about teachers being fired for their social networking presence have caused many teachers to take a deep breath and a serious pause before diving into social networking. They are worried that if they say something inappropriate online, they may face discipline or even lose their job. No doubt, this is a serious concern.

Like many slippery slopes, however, this one covers a wide swath of ground. There is a big difference between participating in a learning network and saying something so inappropriate that it prompts your dismissal. In essence, the rules online are not that much different from the rules in face-to-face situations: don't share excessive personal information, and don't post anything online that you wouldn't be comfortable discussing with your principal, your colleagues, or your parents and students.

If a person is really afraid of making a misstep, set up a buddy system with another teacher or staff member to review his or her online contributions. Have the buddy look at the person's tweets, blog posts, and other contributions for a few weeks and give feedback on tone and content. At the same time, have the person critique the feeds of other users in a dialogue about appropriate professional content. These small interactions will build the confidence needed to work without a net.

Closing In on the Finish Line

Whatever path you take toward bringing the tools and the access for networked learning to your students, know this: the path will be filled with turns and forks and potholes. It may seem at times as if nothing is changing, everyone is upset, and none of the technology or ideas will work. We know it's easy to say, but trust the process. In *The Six Secrets of Change*, Michael Fullan points out that organizations going through a change experience an "implementation dip," a time when the behaviors change but the beliefs don't (Fullan, 2008). Often it feels like things are getting worse, not better. In order for the change to succeed, you will need to weather the storm of this turbulent time and come out on the other side.

Remember, your community will need to travel through the transformation stages that we outlined in chapters 2, 3, and 4 for students to fully reap the rewards. Be patient, and keep in mind that there really is no other alternative. Our students need to learn in networks, and therefore, we do, too. It doesn't matter how long it takes. Every movement forward is one more step on the path to the future. That's what really matters.

EPILOGUE

THE FUTURE OF SCHOOLING

Throughout this book, our aim has been to describe the transformative power of networked learning and to give you the practical strategies you need to begin a meaningful process of change for your schools and, more importantly, for yourselves. We know we haven't answered every question or dealt with every possible scenario of change. Every school will travel down this path in a different way. We do hope, however, you feel you have a solid foundation for beginning the important and difficult work of rethinking learning for our students. We also hope we've motivated you to act sooner rather than later. If you're feeling challenged, maybe a bit scared, but in general excited about the prospects, we've done our job.

We don't blame you if you're squinting a bit in trying to see where all of this ends up. As we've pointed out, the rise of the web only dates back to 1995 or so, and the rise of learning networks is even shorter. So much has become possible for our learning in such a short period of time that one can't help but wonder at the startling implications as we stare five, ten, or twenty years down the road. Learning on the web is in its infancy. Trying to envision its effect on schools a couple of decades from now is like trying to predict the Internet a few moments after the first telephone call. But some trends are emerging, and we'd like to take these last few pages to discuss what those larger themes might be.

Perhaps the easiest one to see on the horizon is the continued explosion of mobile computing. It is not a stretch to say that in as little as ten years, every student will have a personal Internet-enabled device available to them constantly as part of their educational experience, and some would say that's a pretty conservative estimate. We've said this before—by itself, that device doesn't do much. What really counts is the power to plug into networks for learning under the guidance of a teacher who knows how to do that. But access is a start. When every student is connected, things start to get interesting. As Clay Shirky wrote in his book *Here Comes Everybody*, "tools don't get socially interesting until they get technologically boring . . . It's when a technology becomes normal, then ubiquitous, and finally so pervasive as to be invisible, that the really profound changes happen" (2008). We said it before: buckle up. The real shifts haven't yet started.

Ubiquitous access via mobile devices will create schools in which students reach out to teachers from around the world to build networks for their own learning as routinely as they currently take notes in a notebook. They won't

do this as something novel or new, but as a central methodology in their learning. Right now, most students still think about learning as local, as something that happens when they are in school with access to textbooks and instructions from a teacher. In the future, when they are sitting at the center of a web of connections that never shuts down, learning will seem more fluid, more constant, and less constrained, and their teachers will seem like the most important part of understanding how to leverage the power of this network.

That will require an evolution in the role of the teacher—from a content specialist who dispenses knowledge as a commodity to a classroom facilitator who helps students grow the skills for their own learning. Once again, this is not a new goal for educators, but it is newly possible when content is more easily accessible and lifelong learning begins to evolve into a set of skills for reaching outside the four walls of the classroom. Teachers will have a broader, more interdisciplinary role that looks more like the discovery mode now appearing in the classrooms of teachers like Clarence Fisher, Anne Smith, Brian Crosby, Shelley Wright, and Shannon Miller and in entire schools like Hunterdon Central and Science Leadership Academy. It's nearly impossible for one teacher to go deep with thirty students, but it is possible for one teacher to help students go deep using dozens of other teachers.

One of the things that will make this depth possible is the continued ability to personalize learning for our students. Individualization of content and instruction is a lofty goal that stretches back to John Dewey and beyond, but the technological explosion puts it more in reach than at any other time. In the same way that people dreamed about going into space for hundreds of years before the science made it possible, teachers have dreamed about students learning at their own pace within learning paths customized for them. Now, for the first time, the web enables them to break the gravity of mass instruction. In the not-too-distant future, the web will be able to deliver content around our interests and needs before we even ask for it. If there is a tangible threat to education as we know it, it may be the many businesses that are beginning to create ways to help us learn without school. One of our greatest fears, in fact, is that those with the means to do so will opt out of schools in favor of services that can provide more customized, passion-based learning paths for kids.

Either way, the days of the static paper textbook are numbered as each student will soon access dynamic content in real time, often in immersive environments of virtual reality. Simulations have enormous potential to change how we think of learning, particularly when they are web enabled and involve thousands of people from around the world. We're not talking about World of Warcraft, but rather things like World Without Oil, a massive simulation that took place online with people from all continents as a learning exercise to predict the results of a worldwide oil shortage. Closer to home, students can explore potential career paths through simulations that allow them to be a lawyer or doctor for a day. All of these simulations use the power of games to engage students in a learning dynamic that provides just enough challenge to encourage growth and mastery.

These changes will cause a huge premium to be put on teachers as learners. In the future, teachers' networks will actively inform every instructional decision every day. Transparent sharing of content and instruction will mean that teachers can dip into a torrent of connections to grab the strategies they need in their classrooms. A continuous global dialogue of teachers will ensure that the best methods for supporting teaching and learning are freely available, along with the evidence of their effectiveness.

Taken together, we hope that by 2020 schools will have evolved into real centers of learning, the most important node in a student's expanding learning network. We can imagine schools as places where younger students are steeped in exploration, problem solving, performance, art, and collaboration, and where older students are given the license to own their learning, pursue their passions, and become expert learners under the watchful eye of mentor teacher-learners. We can imagine the end of age groupings, of distinct disciplines, and to some extent, the current school calendar and schedule as we begin to think about our learning as something we carry with us constantly. Schools become places where teachers help students manage these networks, where students build capacity and create meaningful, beautiful work that is shared with the world on a regular basis. They become places where children are in the presence of caring, nurturing adults who guide them and push them to be the best learners and human beings they can possibly be by leveraging the power of connections.

No doubt, our kids will still share deep and rich learning experiences with other children and adults in their local communities, experience the profound benefits of working with others side by side to create meaningful and excellent work, perform for local audiences, and know the pride and satisfaction that comes with it. Our schools will play an important role in making all of that happen, but they will also be places that push our kids out into this new virtual space in equally profound ways, making sure every child has the opportunity to learn deeply and experience the beauty and the complexity of the world in which we live.

We'll finish with this: regardless of where we and our children find ourselves in twenty years, we hope that educators have been the driving force of whatever changes we've made. For that vision of a better, more relevant, more engaging education to be realized for our children, each one of us must make a commitment to change, to learn, and to expand our own conception of what teaching and learning and schooling looks like.

It is an amazing time to be a learner. For our kids' sakes, seize the moment; start your own journey. Lead. Our sincere best wishes along the way.

REFERENCES AND RESOURCES

Ahrens, F. (2009, October 27). The accelerating decline of newspapers. *Washington Post*. Accessed at www.washingtonpost.com/wp-dyn /content/article/2009/10/26/AR2009102603272.html on February 24, 2011.

Alcorn, A. (n.d.). *The very unofficial Facebook privacy manual*. Accessed at http://manuals.makeuseof.com.s3.amazonaws.com/FacebookPrivacy .pdf on February 24, 2011.

Anderson, J., & Bernoff, J. (2010, September 28). *A global update of social technographics: An* empowered *report: Social media growth is centered on social networking* [Research report]. Cambridge, MA: Forrester Research.

Anderson, J., & Rainie, L. (2010). *Millennials will make online sharing in networks a lifelong habit*. Washington, DC: Pew Research Center. Accessed at www.pewinternet.org/Reports/2010/Future-of -Millennials.aspx on February 24, 2011.

Arapahoe High School. (n.d.). A whole new learning experience [video file]. Accessed at http://video.google.com/videoplay?docid=-5095321483555 768631&hl=en# on February 24, 2011.

Arnsdorff, M., & Carroll, J. (2009, June 23). Mounting research reveals alarming danger associated with improper backpack use [Web log post]. Accessed at http://backpacksafety.blogspot.com/2009/06 /mounting-research-reveals-alarming.html on February 24, 2011.

Ayres, I. (2010a). *Carrots and sticks* [Kindle version]. New York: Bantam.

Ayers, I. (2010b). Carrots and sticks has landed. Accessed at www.law.yale .edu/news/12290.htm on March 18, 2011.

Bauerlein, M. (2008). *The dumbest generation: How the digital age stupefies young Americans and jeopardizes our future*. New York: Penguin.

Bernoff, J. (2010, January 19). Social technographics: Conversationalists get onto the ladder [Web log post]. Accessed at http://forrester.typepad .com/groundswell/2010/01/conversationalists-get-onto-the-ladder .html on February 11, 2011.

Bingham, T., & Conner, M. (2010). *New social learning* [Kindle version]. Alexandria, VA: American Society for Training & Development.

Breck, J. (2010, December 16). Mobile-only web use surging worldwide [Web log post]. Accessed at http://handschooling.com/2010/12/16/mobile -only-web-use-surging-worldwide on February 24, 2011.

Brockman, J. (2010). How is the Internet changing the way you think? In *Edge: World question center*. Accessed at www.edge.org/q2010/q10_index .html on February 15, 2011.

Brown, J. S., & Adler, R. P. (2008). Minds on fire: Open education, the long tail, and learning 2.0. *EDUCAUSE Review, 43*(1), 16–38. Accessed at www.educause.edu/EDUCAUSE+Review/EDUCAUSEReviewMagazine Volume43/MindsonFireOpenEducationtheLon/162420 on February 24, 2011.

Carr, N. (2010). *The shallows: What the Internet is doing to our brains.* New York: W. W. Norton & Company.

Chadwick, K., & Gore, J. (2010). *Globaloria pilot study: The relationship of Globaloria participation and student achievement.* Charleston, WV: Edvantia. Accessed at http://worldwideworkshop.org/pdfs/Globaloria ReportFinal020310.pdf on February 24, 2011.

Chamberlain, W. (n.d.). *Mr. C's class blog.* Accessed at http://mrcsclassblog.blogspot.com on February 24, 2011.

City of Minneapolis. (2010). *Wireless Minneapolis.* Accessed at www.ci .minneapolis.mn.us/wirelessminneapolis on February 24, 2011.

Couros, A. (2011, March 7). Excellent intro. to Twitter by the amazing @nancywhite on Vimeo http://t.co/RiK815B via @Diigo [Twitter post]. Accessed at http://twitter.com/courosa/statuses/44818726708711424 on March 17, 2011.

Crosby, B. (2008). Inclusion [Video file]. Accessed at www.arisleyschool.org /Inclusion.mov on February 24, 2011.

Crosby, B. (2010). *Learning is messy.* Accessed at http://learningismessy.com on February 24, 2011.

Cross, J. (2006). *Informal learning.* San Francisco: Pfeiffer.

Cybrary Man. (n.d.). Educational hash tags. *Cybrary man's educational web sites.* Accessed at www.cybraryman.com/edhashtags.html on February 24, 2011.

de la Merced, M. (2010, September 23). Blockbuster, hoping to reinvent itself, files for bankruptcy. *New York Times.* Accessed at www.nytimes .com/2010/09/24/business/24blockbuster.html?_r=1&src=busln on February 24, 2011.

Deutschman, A. (2007). *Change or die: The three keys to change at work and in life.* New York: HarperCollins.

Downes, S. (2010, October 18). A world to change. *Huffington Post.* Accessed at www.huffingtonpost.com/stephen-downes/a-world-to-change_b _762738.html on February 24, 2011.

Dweck, C. (2006). *Mindset: The new psychology of success.* New York: Random House.

edutopia. (2011, March 7). New! Strategies for Embedding Project-Based Learning into #STEM http://bit.ly/fAaotB #scichat #edchat [Twitter post]. Accessed at http://twitter.com/edutopia/status/448 65384997847040 on March 17, 2011.

Elliott, N. (2010, September 28). *European social technographics 2010: The rise of the joiners and the conversationalists* [Research report]. Cambridge, MA: Forrester Research.

eSchool News. (2010, April 21). Survey: Teens' cell phone use may cause tension with parents, schools. *eSchool News*. Accessed at www .eschoolnews.com/2010/04/21/survey-teens-cell-phone-use-may -cause-tension-with-parents-schools on February 8, 2011.

Federal Communications Commission. (2009). *Children's Internet Protection Act*. Accessed at www.fcc.gov/cgb/consumerfacts/cipa.html on February 24, 2011.

Fisher, C. (n.d.). Connecting assessment [Rubric]. Accessed at https://docs .google.com/Doc?docid=0ASE-WviNjA7KZGZzczRweF8zNGZjY2J4M2 Ny&hl=en on February 24, 2011.

Fisher, C. (2006, September 28). I'm hearing voices [Web log post]. Accessed at www.evenfromhere.org/?p=530 on February 24, 2011.

Fullan, M. (2008). *The six secrets of change*. Accessed at www.michaelfullan .ca/resource_assets/handouts/08_Nov_Keynote_A4.pdf on February 24, 2011.

Gray, L., Thomas, N., & Lewis, L. (2010). *Educational technology in U.S. public schools: Fall 2008* (NCES Report No. 2010– 034). Washington, DC: Government Printing Office. Accessed at http://nces.ed.gov/pubs 2010/2010034.pdf on February 24, 2011.

Hagel, J., Brown, J. S., & Davison, L. (2009). Abandon stocks, embrace flows. *Harvard Business Review*. Accessed at http://blogs.hbr.org/bigshift /2009/01/abandon-stocks-embrace-flows.html on March 18, 2011.

Hart, J. (2010). *Final top 100 tools for learning 2010 list*. Accessed at www .c4lpt.co.uk/recommended/top100-2010.html on February 24, 2011.

Heath, C., & Heath, D. (2010). *Switch: How to change things when things are hard* [Kindle version]. New York: Crown Business.

Hernandez, B. (2010, July 8). Pew research: Wealthy have laptops, the poor have cell phones. *PCWorld*. Accessed at www.pcworld.com /article/200726/pew_research_wealthy_have_laptops_the_poor _have_cell_phones.html on February 24, 2011.

Hobson, J. (2009, November 4). Danish pupils use web in exams. *BBC News*. Accessed at http://news.bbc.co.uk/2/hi/uk_news/education/8341886 .stm on February 24, 2011.

Hoffer, E. (n.d.). In times of change . . . [Quote]. Accessed at www.famous quotesabout.com/quote/In-times-of-change/100918 on February 24, 2011.

International Society for Technology in Education. (2009). NETS for administrators 2009. Accessed at www.iste.org/standards/nets-for -administrators/nets-for-administrators-sandards.aspx on February 24, 2011.

Ito, M., Horst, H., Bittanti, M., boyd, d., Herr-Stephenson, B., Lange, P., et al. (2008). *Living and learning with new media: Summary of findings from the digital youth project* [White paper]. Chicago: MacArthur Foundation. Accessed at http://digitalyouth.ischool.berkeley.edu /files/report/digitalyouth-WhitePaper.pdf on February 24, 2011.

Johnson, L., Levine, A., Smith, R., & Stone, S. (2010). *The 2010 Horizon Report*. Austin, TX: The New Media Consortium. Accessed at www.nmc.org /pdf/2010-Horizon-Report.pdf on February 24, 2011.

Kohn, A. (2010, September 19). Schools would be great if it weren't for the kids. *Washington Post*. Accessed at http://voices.washingtonpost.com /answer-sheet/guest-bloggers/schools-would-be-great-if-it-w .html#more on February 24, 2011.

Kotter. J. (1995). *Leading change* [Kindle version]. Boston: Harvard Business.

Kuropatwa, D. (2006, November 21). Distributed teaching and learning [Web blog post]. Accessed at http://adifference.blogspot.com/2006/11 /distributed-teaching-and-learning_21.html on February 24, 2011.

Leadbeater, C., & Wong, A. (2010). *Learning from the extremes* [White paper]. Accessed at www.cisco.com/web/about/citizenship/socio-economic /docs/LearningfromExtremes_WhitePaper.pdf on February 24, 2011.

Lee, L. (2010). Fostering reflective writing and interactive exchange through blogging in an advanced language course. *ReCALL, 22*(02), 212–227. Accessed at http://journals.cambridge.org/action/displayAbstract?from Page=online&aid=7798112 on February 24, 2011.

Lenhart, A., Smith, A., Purcell, K., & Zickuhr, K. (2011). *Social media and young adults*. Washington, DC: Pew Research Center. Accessed at http://pewinternet.org/Reports/2010/Social-Media-and-Young-Adults /Part-3/1-Teens-and-online-social-networks.aspx?r=1 on February 24, 2011.

MacArthur Foundation. (2008, November 20). New study shows time spent online important for teen development [Press release]. Accessed at www.macfound.org/site/c.lkLXJ8MQKrH/b.4773437/k.3CE6/New _Study_Shows_Time_Spent_Online_Important_for_Teen_Development .htm on February 24, 2011.

Mardis, M., Everhart, N., Smith, D., Newsum, J., & Baker, S. (2010). *From paper to pixel: Digital textbooks and Florida schools* [White paper]. Accessed at www.palmcenter.fsu.edu/documents/digitaltextbooks_whitepaper .pdf on February 24, 2011.

Martinez, S. (2010, October 21) Not enough tech support = no technology use [Web log post]. Accessed at http://blog.genyes.org/indexphp/2010 /10/21/not-enough-tech-support-no-technology-use on February 24, 2011.

McBride, R., & King, V. (2010). Improving writing skills using blogging in the elementary classroom: Choosing tools they use. In D. Gibson & B. Dodge (Eds.), *Proceedings of Society for Information Technology & Teacher Education International Conference 2010* (pp. 2768–2774). Chesapeake, VA: Association for the Advancement of Computing in Education.

McNaughton, M. (2011, March 7). 80% of U.S. teens will use social networks by 2011. *Realtime Report.* Accessed at http://twtrcon.com/2011/03/07/80-of-u-s-teens-will-use-social-networks-in-2011/ on March 12, 2011.

Miller, R. (2005, November 30). A recipe for newspaper survival in the internet age [Web log post]. Accessed at http://slashdot.org/articles/05/11/27/1645214.shtml on February 24, 2011.

Miller, S. (2010a). Welcome to the Web 2.0/PLN course! Accessed at https://docs.google.com/documentd/1esjD5jLMu1Fk1lsGSU3jv0BNqEU_KoZ1ox7C9VpDA5c/edit?hl=en# on April 8, 2010.

Miller, S. (2010b). Web 2.0/PLN course. *Mrs. Miller's Voice.* Accessed at https://sites.google.com/a/vmbulldogs.com/shannon-miller/courses-i-teach/web-2-0-pln-course on February 24, 2011.

Mitra, S. (2010). The child-driven education [Video file]. Accessed at www.ted.com/talks/lang/eng/sugata_mitra_the_child_driven_education.html on February 24, 2011.

Nash, S. (2011). *St. Joseph Digital Express.* Accessed at http://saintjosephschools.ning.com on February 17, 2010.

National Council of Teachers of English. (2008). NCTE framework for 21st century curriculum and assessment. Accessed at www.ncte.org/governance/21stcenturyframework?source=gs on February 24, 2011.

Natural Resources Defense Council. (n.d.). The green squad. Accessed at www.nrdc.org/greensquad/intro/intro_1.asp on March 18, 2011.

Newspaper Association of America. (2011). Total paid circulation [Spreadsheet]. Accessed at www.naa.org/TrendsandNumbers/Total-Paid-Circulation.aspx on February 7, 2011.

NPR. (2010). Digital overload: Your brain on gadgets. Accessed at www.npr.org/templates/story/story.php?storyId=129384107 on March 7, 2011.

OECD. (2010). Figure 1: Comparing countries' and economies' performance [Spreadsheet]. Accessed at www.pisa.oecd.org/dataoecd/54/12/46643496.pdf on February 7, 2011.

P2P Foundation. (2007). Networked proximity. Accessed at http://p2pfoundation.net/Networked_Proximity on February 8, 2011.

Pesce, M. (2008, December 6). Fluid learning [Web log post]. Accessed at http://blog.futurestreetconsulting.com/?p=94 on February 24, 2011.

Peters, T. (1999, April 30). The wow project. *Fast Company.* Accessed at www
.fastcompany.com/magazine/24/wowproj.html on February 24, 2011.

Powers, W. (2010). *Hamlet's blackberry: A practical philosophy for building a good
life in the digital age.* New York: HarperCollins.

Project RED. (2010). *Project RED key findings: Revolutionizing education*
[Presentation]. Accessed at www.projectred.org/uploads/ISTE%20
2010%20Presentation%20v2.pdf on March 18, 2011.

Project Tomorrow. (2010). *Unleashing the future: Educators "speak up" about the
use of emerging technologies for learning.* Accessed at www.tomorrow.org
/speakup/pdfs/SU09UnleashingTheFuture.pdf on February 24, 2011.

Reynolds, G. (2005, October 7). The "Lessig Method" of presentation [Web log
post]. Accessed at http://presentationzen.blogs.com/presentationzen
/2005/10/the_lessig_meth.html on February 24, 2011.

Rheingold, H. (2009, April 20). Attention literacy. *SFGate.* Accessed at www
.sfgate.com/cgi-bin/blogs/rheingold/detail?entry_id=38828 on
February 24, 2011.

Richardson, W. (2008). Footprints in the digital age. *Educational Leadership,
66*(3), 16–19. Accessed at www.ascd.org/publications/educational
-leadership/nov08/vol66/num03/Footprints-in-the-Digital-Age.aspx
on February 24, 2011.

richhoward. (2010). The Internet in 2020 [Graphic]. Accessed at www.intac
.net/the-internet-in-2020 on February 17, 2011.

Robinson, K. (2010, February). Bring on the learning revolution [Video file].
Accessed at www.ted.com/talks/sir_ken_robinson_bring_on_the
_revolution.html on February 24, 2011.

Roblimo. (2005, November 30). *A recipe for newspaper survival in the Internet age.*
Accessed at http://slashdot.org/story/05/11/27/1645214/A-Recipe-for
-Newspaper-Survival-in-the-Internet-Age on February 7, 2011.

Scola, N. (2010, December 9). Pew: Twitter's your place for news [Web log
post]. Accessed at http://techpresident.com/blog-entry/pew
-twitters-your-place-news on February 24, 2011.

Shirky, C. (2008). *Here comes everybody: The power of organizing without
organizations* [Kindle version]. New York: Penguin Press.

Shirky, C. (2010). *Cognitive surplus: Creativity and generosity in a connected age*
[Kindle version]. New York: Penguin Press.

Siemens, G. (2007). Learning. Accessed at http://ltc.umanitoba.ca/wikis
/KnowingKnowledge/index.php/Learning on February 24, 2011.

Siemens, G. (2010, February 16). Teaching in social and technological
networks [Web log post]. Accessed at www.connectivism.ca/?p=220
%29 on February 24, 2011.

Smith, A. (2010a, September 9). Alfie Kohn—I need you [Web log post]. Accessed at http://learningandlaptops.blogspot.com/2010/09/alfie -kohn-i-need-you.html on February 24, 2011.

Smith, A. (2010b, September 29). A conversation to improve [Web log post]. Accessed at http://learningandlaptops.blogspot.com/2010/09 /conversation-to-improve.html on February 24, 2011.

Smith, A. (2010c, October 14). This I Believe goes global 10-11 [Web log post]. Accessed at http://learningandlaptops.blogspot.com/2010/10/this-i -believe-goes-global-10-11.html on February 24, 2011.

Stansbury, M. (2008, January 9). Schools need help with tech support. *eSchools News*. Accessed at www.eschoolnews.com/2008/01/09/schools -need-help-with-tech-support on February 24, 2011.

Stevens, V. (2009). Modeling social media in groups, communities, and networks. *TESL-EJ*, *13*(3). Accessed at www.tesl-ej.org/wordpress /issues/volume13/ej51/ej51int on February 24, 2011.

Stock, E., & Fisman, R. (2010, October 22). The not-so-simple debate on home computers and achievement. *Huffington Post*. Accessed at www .huffingtonpost.com/elisabeth-stock/the-notsosimple-debate -on_b_772620.html on February 24, 2011.

Stone, B. (2009, January 13). Report calls online threats to children overblown. *New York Times*. Accessed at www.nytimes.com/2009 /01/14/technology/internet/14cyberweb.html?_r=1 on February 24, 2011.

Stone, L. (2010, July 24). Continuous partial attention—Not the same as multi-tasking. *Business Week*. Accessed at www.businessweek.com /business_at_work/time_management/archives/2008/07/continuous _part.html on February 24, 2011.

Sydell, L. (2010, July 8). Stanford ushers in the age of bookless libraries. *National Public Radio*. Accessed at www.npr.org/templates/story/story .php?storyId=128361395 on February 24, 2011.

TEDxTalks, (2010a, July 19). Brian Crosby—Back to the future [Video file]. Accessed at www.youtube.com/watch?v=66mrAzz7nLw on February 24, 2011.

TEDxTalks. (2010b, October 12). Michael Wesch—From knowledgeable to knowledge-able. [Video file]. Accessed at www.youtube.com/watch?v =LeaAHv4UTI8&feature=player_embedded#! on February 24, 2011.

United States Department of Education. (2010a). *National Education Technology Plan 2010*. Accessed at www.ed.gov/technology/netp-2010 on February 24, 2011.

United States Department of Education. (2010b). *Transforming American education: Learning powered by technology*. Accessed at www.ed.gov/sites /default/files/netp2010-execsumm.pdf on February 24, 2011.

United States Department of Education. (2010c). *An evaluation of evidence-based practices in online learning: A meta-analysis and review of online learning studies.* Accessed at www2.ed.gov/rschstat/eval/tech/evidence-based -practices/finalreport.pdf on February 24, 2011.

Wagner, T. (2010). *The global achievement gap: Why even our best schools don't teach the new survival skills our children need—And what we can do about it* [Kindle version]. New York: Basic Books.

Weigel, M., James, C., & Gardner, H. (2009). Learning: Peering backward and looking forward in the digital era. *International Journal of Learning and Media, 1*(1), 1–18. Accessed at www.mitpressjournals.org/doi/pdf/10 .1162/ijlm.2009.0005 on February 24, 2011.

Wesch, M. (2009, January 7). From knowledgeable to knowledge-able: Learning in new media environments. *Academic Commons.* Accessed at www.academiccommons.org/commons/essay/knowledgable -knowledge-able on February 24, 2011.

Wiley, D. (2008). Openness and the disaggregated future of higher education [Powerpoint slides]. Accessed at www.slideshare.net/opencontent /openness-and-the-disaggregated-future-of-higher-education -presentation on February 24, 2011.

Wright, S. (2010a, October 6). Loss [Web log post]. Accessed at http:// shelleywright.wordpress.com/2010/10/26/loss on February 24, 2011.

Wright, S. (2010b, November 11). Taking the plunge [Web log post]. Accessed at http://shelleywright.wordpress.com/2010/11/21/taking-the-plunge on February 24, 2011.

Young, J. R. (2010, October 24). To save students money, colleges may force a switch to e-textbooks. *Chronicle of Higher Education.* Accessed at http:// chronicle.com/article/The-End-of-the-Textbook-as-We/125044 on February 16, 2011.

YouTube. (n.d.). YouTube fact sheet. Accessed at www.youtube.com/t/fact _sheet on February 8, 2011.

INDEX